ML
YA

STAR WARS®
DARK TIMES

VOLUME FOUR

BLUE HARVEST

THE RISE OF THE EMPIRE

From 1,000 to 0 years before the battle of Yavin

After the seeming final defeat of the Sith, the Republic enters a state of complacency.
In the waning years of the Republic, the Senate rife with corruption, the ambitious
Senator Palpatine causes himself to be elected Supreme Chancellor.
This is the era of the prequel trilogy.

The events in this story take place approximately nineteen years before
the Battle of Yavin (three months after the events in *Revenge of the Sith*).

STAR WARS®
DARK TIMES

VOLUME FOUR

BLUE HARVEST

Script
MICK HARRISON

Art
DOUGLAS WHEATLEY

Colors
DAVE McCAIG
CHRIS CHUCKRY
DAN JACKSON

Lettering
MICHAEL HEISLER

Front Cover Art
DOUGLAS WHEATLEY
colored by
DAVE McCAIG

Back Cover Art
DUSTIN WEAVER
from a drawing by
DOUGLAS WHEATLEY

DARK HORSE BOOKS®

President and Publisher
MIKE RICHARDSON

Collection Designer
TONY ONG

Editor
RANDY STRADLEY

Assistant Editor
FREDDYE LINS

Mike Richardson President and Publisher • **Neil Hankerson** Executive Vice President • **Tom Weddle** Chief Financial Officer • **Randy Stradley** Vice President of Publishing • **Michael Martens** Vice President of Business Development • **Anita Nelson** Vice President of Business Affairs • **Micha Hershman** Vice President of Marketing • **David Scroggy** Vice President of Product Development • **Dale LaFountain** Vice President of Information Technology • **Darlene Vogel** Director of Purchasing • **Ken Lizzi** General Counsel • **Cara Niece** Director of Scheduling • **Scott Allie** Senior Managing Editor • **Chris Warner** Senior Books Editor • **Diana Schutz** Executive Editor • **Cary Grazzini** Director of Design and Production • **Lia Ribacchi** Art Director • **Davey Estrada** Editorial Director

special thanks to Jann Moorhead, David Anderman, Troy Alders, Leland Chee, Sue Rostoni, and Carol Roeder at Lucas Licensing

STAR WARS: DARK TIMES Volume Four—Blue Harvest

This volume collects *Dark Times: Blue Harvest* #0 and issues #13 through #17 of the Dark Horse comic-book series *Star Wars: Dark Times*.

Published by
Dark Horse Books
A division of Dark Horse Comics, Inc.
10956 SE Main Street
Milwaukie, OR 97222

darkhorse.com
starwars.com

To find a comics shop in your area, call the Comic Shop Locator Service
toll-free at 1-888-266-4226

First edition: November 2010
ISBN 978-1-59582-264-2

Library of Congress Cataloging-in-Publication Data

Star Wars. Dark Times / script Mick Harrison ; art Douglas Wheatley ; colors Dave McCaig, Chris Chuckry, Dan Jackson ; letters Michael Heisler ; front cover art Douglas Wheatley ; back cover art Dustin Weaver ; from a drawing by Douglas Wheatley.
  v. cm.
Contents: v. 4. Blue harvest (six issues of a comic-book series)
Description based on v. 4, published in 2010. Vol. 1 published in 2008.
ISBN 978-1-59582-264-2
1. Star Wars fiction--Comic books, strips, etc. 2. Graphic novels. I. Harrison, Mick. II. Wheatley, Doug. III. Chuckry, Chris. IV. Title: Dark times, Star Wars.
PN6728.S73S524 2010
741.5'973--dc22
                  2009049793

1 3 5 7 9 10 8 6 4 2
Printed at Midas Printing International, Ltd., Huizhou, China

**"FOR OVER A THOUSAND GENERATIONS, THE JEDI KNIGHTS WERE THE GUARDIANS OF PEACE AND JUSTICE IN THE OLD REPUBLIC. BEFORE THE DARK TIMES, BEFORE THE EMPIRE."
—BEN KENOBI**

At the end of the Clone Wars, Chancellor Palpatine's Order 66 resulted in the destruction of the Jedi Order and the scattering of its few survivors. Dass Jennir is one of those survivors. Abandoned by his companions after a failed attempt to rescue his friend Bomo Greenbark's wife and daughter, Jennir is seeking a new path for himself in a galaxy now under Imperial rule.

In a time when all Jedi are considered outlaws, can Jennir live like an outlaw without actually becoming one?

Art by
DOUGLAS WHEATLEY

CATO NEIMOIDIA, THE "BRIDGE WORLD." ONCE A SEAT OF POWER OF THE NEIMOIDIAN COLONIES AND THE TRADE FEDERATION, IN THE AFTERMATH OF THE CLONE WARS IT IS A PLANET RIPE FOR PLUNDER...

...ATTRACTING SCAVENGERS AND GRIFTERS FROM AROUND THE GALAXY.

INCLUDING ONE CALLED DASS JENNIR...

...A JEDI KNIGHT. OR, HE WAS UNTIL THE EMPIRE WIPED OUT THE JEDI ORDER. NOW...

WHAT IS HE NOW?

THEY SAY A MAN IS THE **SUM** OF ALL OF HIS EXPERIENCES, BUT JENNIR FEELS LIKE HIS RECENT HISTORY HAS BEEN A SERIES OF **SUBTRACTIONS.**

IT BEGAN WHEN THE JEDI WERE BETRAYED BY THE TROOPS THEY HAD COMMANDED.

SIDING WITH THE NOSAURIANS TO FIGHT THE NEWLY FOUNDED EMPIRE LED TO A DISASTROUS DEFEAT...NOT ONLY FOR HIMSELF, BUT FOR ALL THE NOSAURIANS -- INCLUDING HIS FRIEND **BOMO GREENBARK.**

AND JOINING THE OUTLAW CREW OF THE SHIP **UHUMELE** TO RESCUE BOMO'S ENSLAVED FAMILY...

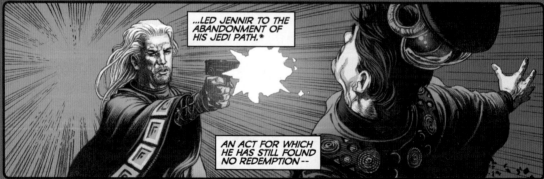

...LED JENNIR TO THE ABANDONMENT OF HIS JEDI PATH.*

AN ACT FOR WHICH HE HAS STILL FOUND NO REDEMPTION --

-- AND WHICH SAVED NEITHER BOMO'S WIFE AND CHILD, NOR THEIR FRIENDSHIP.

WHAT HE IS, IS ALONE...

10

* As seen in *Star Wars: Dark Times – The Path to Nowhere.*

...AND BROKE.

EVEN A FUGITIVE JEDI NEEDS TO EAT. WHICH IS WHAT BROUGHT HIM HERE --

HE SENSES HER BEFORE HE SEES HER...

...AND HE CATCHES HER SCENT A SECOND AFTER THAT. AN AROMA THAT SPEAKS OF SOFTNESS AND WARMTH...WITH THE TANG OF SOMETHING SPICY.

EVERYONE ELSE IN THE CANTINA PICKS UP ON THE SAME UNSPOKEN MESSAGE --

-- A NEW JOB HAS OPENED UP.

JENNIR HAD HEARD THE CANTINA WAS THE PLACE TO FIND OFF-THE-RECORD JOBS. NO HOLOFEEDS, NO REMOTES. EVERY JOB OFFER IS POSTED DIRECTLY BY THE CLIENT --

-- A CLOSED SYSTEM FOR HIRING MERCENARIES, SMUGGLERS, AND OTHER TROUBLESHOOTERS...

...NOTHING TO ALERT THE EMPIRE.

THUS FAR, THOUGH, JENNIR HAS NOT FOUND A JOB HIS JEDI SCRUPLES WILL ALLOW HIM TO ACCEPT.

PERHAPS THIS ONE WILL BE...DIFFERENT...

MY NAME IS EMBER CHANKELI. I NEED A WARRIOR...

...OR A SECURITY OFFICER TO HELP ME WITH A GANG PROBLEM...

SHE GOES ON TO SAY THAT SHE WANTS SOMEONE WHO CAN RID HER TOWN OF A GANG -- BY GUILE OR BY FORCE -- TO RESTORE IT TO WHAT IT ONCE WAS...

...TO MAKE THE TOWN SAFE ONCE MORE FOR ITS CITIZENS. THIS IS A JOB JENNIR CAN FEEL COMFORTABLE ACCEPTING. AND IT PAYS WELL, TOO.

HE MAKES A NOTE OF THE TIME AND PLACE TO MEET...

THAT JOB IS MINE!

I'M CERTAIN THE LADY WILL MAKE HER CHOICE...

I SAID THE JOB'S MINE!

JENNIR'S ADVERSARY IS A CHISTORI. REPTILE TOUGH...REPTILE FAST...

...REPTILE STUPID.

REPTILE ANGRY.

UHHN...

STAY DOWN.

YOU MAKE FRIENDS WHEREVER YOU GO, DON'T YOU?

SHUT UP, *H2.*

WHATEVER YOU SAY, MAN-WHO-KILLED-MY-MASTER.

WHERE ARE WE GOING?

BACK TO THE SHIP. I HAVE AN APPOINTMENT WITH A LADY IN THE MORNING.

TRY YOUR LUCK AT SABACC, PILGRIM!

MASTER KAI HUDORRA -- ANOTHER SURVIVOR OF THE CLONES' BETRAYAL -- PLANNED TO MAKE HIS LIVING AS A GAMBLER...

...USING THE **FORCE** TO MANIPULATE THE OUTCOME OF THE GAMES. JENNIR IS CERTAIN THAT HUDORRA IS DOING WELL, SOMEWHERE OUT IN THE GALAXY.

LOSER.

THAT PATH IS NOT FOR JENNIR. HIS JEDI IDEALS -- SERVICE TO THE FORCE AND THE GREATER GOOD -- ARE ALL HE HAS LEFT.

THOUGH, ADHERENCE TO THOSE PRINCIPLES DESTROYED WHATEVER FRIENDSHIP HE HAD WITH BOMO GREENBARK...

...AND THEY DO LITTLE TO PUT FOOD ON HIS PLATE OR FUEL IN THE SHIP HE "INHERITED" FROM H2'S LATE MASTER, THE CANNIBAL SLAVER DEZONO QUA.

BUT TOMORROW HIS LUCK MAY CHANGE.

A BRIGHT, CLEAR MORNING -- UNUSUAL FOR CATO NEIMOIDIA.

SOME MIGHT TAKE IT AS AN OMEN, BUT JEDI-IN-HIDING *DASS JENNIR* HAS OTHER CONCERNS...

YOU LIKE HER, DON'T YOU?

STAY WITH THE SHIP, *H2.*

YOU MEAN *THIS* SHIP, THAT ONCE BELONGED TO MY *MASTER?* OF COURSE.

I CAN BUT DO THE BIDDING OF THE MAN WHO *MURDERED* HIM.

I SAW THE WOMAN LEAVING THE CLUB LAST NIGHT. MY DATA BANKS INDICATE THAT SHE IS NOT UNATTRACTIVE FOR ONE OF YOUR SPECIES.

YOU COULD DO WORSE.

THE DROID, H2, IS A POOR SUBSTITUTE FOR A REAL FRIEND -- THOUGH IT IS THE **ONLY** SUBSTITUTE JENNIR HAS...

...HIS PREVIOUS FRIENDS HAVING ABANDONED HIM WHEN THEY DISCOVERED HE WAS A JEDI.

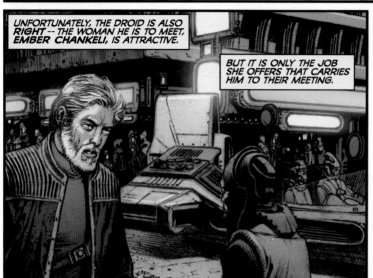

UNFORTUNATELY, THE DROID IS ALSO **RIGHT** -- THE WOMAN HE IS TO MEET, EMBER CHANKELI, IS ATTRACTIVE.

BUT IT IS ONLY THE JOB SHE OFFERS THAT CARRIES HIM TO THEIR MEETING.

HE REMINDS HIMSELF OF THAT AGAIN WHEN HE SEES HER A FEW MOMENTS LATER...

OH, HELLO!

ARE YOU HERE FOR THE JOB, TOO?

THAT DEPENDS ON WHAT THE JOB IS --

YEAH-- YOU WEREN'T VERY SPECIFIC IN YOUR AD.

A GIRL'S GOT TO BE CAREFUL...

I'M FROM A PLACE--A TOWN--THAT DID MOST OF ITS BUSINESS IN THE TOURIST TRADE. THEN A GANG MOVED IN AND MADE THE TOWN ITS HEADQUARTERS. NOW MOST OF THE BUSINESSES ARE FAILING--MINE INCLUDED.

I WANT TO PUT THINGS BACK THE WAY THEY WERE ...BEFORE THE GANG.

HOW MANY IN THIS GANG?

ABOUT FORTY--

FORTY! AND YOU EXPECT THE TWO OF US TO TAKE THEM ON?!

NOT DIRECTLY. BUT THERE'S A WAY YOU CAN JOIN THE GANG --

--SOW DISSENSION FROM WITHIN...MAYBE DRIVE A WEDGE BETWEEN THE BOSS AND HIS CHIEF ENFORCER...

STILL TWO AGAINST FORTY. IT'S IMPOSSIBLE!

BUT ONE AGAINST FORTY MIGHT NOT BE...

I TOLD YOU THIS WAS MY JOB!

19

SO YOU DID. BUT I THOUGHT WE HAD ARRIVED AT A DIFFERENT CONCLUSION.

BAH! YESTERDAY YOU TRICKED ME --

-- TODAY I BROUGHT ENOUGH FRIENDS THAT YOUR TRICKS WON'T WORK!

THE WORDS OF JENNIR'S MASTER COME BACK TO HIM FROM ACROSS THE YEARS: "IF YOU CAN'T WALK AWAY FROM A FIGHT...

"...TAKE CONTROL OF IT. FORCE THE ENEMY TO ENGAGE YOU ON YOUR TERMS..."

I SEE. WHEN WILL THE *REST* OF YOUR FRIENDS BE ARRIVING?

RAARR!

"...FOR A RASH ATTACK IS AN *UNBALANCED* ATTACK...

20

"...AND THUS THE OUTCOME OF A BATTLE MAY BE DECIDED BEFORE THE FIRST BLOW IS STRUCK."

SQUAAWK!

AAWWK!

SNAP!

"BUT DON'T FORGET -- THE FORCE IS A POWERFUL ALLY."

UHHN...

I'M SORRY FOR THAT.

WHAT HAPPENED TO THE OTHER GUY -- YOUR OTHER PROSPECT?

HE RAN...

...WHICH IS JUST AS WELL-- I THINK YOU'RE RIGHT.

ABOUT WHAT?

THAT ONE MAN CAN DO THE JOB OF TWO. AT LEAST...THE *RIGHT* MAN CAN.

I HAVEN'T SAID THAT I'LL *TAKE* THE JOB YET.

YET YOU FOUGHT FOR IT JUST NOW.

THAT...

...WELL, I'M NOT SURE *WHAT* THAT WAS. THEY WERE DETERMINED TO FIGHT.

TELL ME MORE ABOUT THIS JOB. YOU SAID THERE'S A WAY FOR ME TO *JOIN* THE GANG?

YES, THEY'VE PUT OUT THE WORD THAT THEY'RE HOLDING RECRUITING TRIALS IN TWO WEEKS. A MAN WITH YOUR SKILLS WON'T HAVE ANY PROBLEM GETTING IN.

BUT YOU CAN'T LET ON THAT YOU KNOW ME. I'LL GET YOU A ROOM AT MY...INN...SO WE'LL BE ABLE TO KEEP EACH OTHER INFORMED ABOUT WHAT'S GOING ON, BUT IN PUBLIC WE MUST BE STRANGERS. IF THE SLAVERS SUSPECT --

SLAVERS?

YES, THEY'VE TAKEN OVER MOST OF THE TOWN --

I'LL TAKE THE JOB.

JUST LIKE THAT? DON'T YOU EVEN WANT TO KNOW WHERE IT IS?

UH, YES-- I MEAN...

LOOK, I NEED THIS JOB -- MORE THAN I WANTED TO ADMIT. I DON'T WANT YOU TO THINK I'M... UNBALANCED.

DON'T WORRY...

...I KNOW WHAT IT'S LIKE TO BE DOWN TO YOUR LAST CREDIT. BUT IF YOU *ARE "UNBALANCED,"* IT WOULDN'T SURPRISE ME. YOU'D ALMOST *HAVE* TO BE TO TAKE ON FIFTY SLAVERS!

FIFTY? YOU SAID *FORTY* BEFORE...

DID I? MY MISTAKE.

HERE, THE COORDINATES ARE ON THE DATA CHIP.

THESE CREDITS WILL COVER YOUR EXPENSES UNTIL WE MEET AGAIN IN TWO WEEKS...I DON'T KNOW YOUR NAME...

DASS JENNIR.

THANK YOU, DASS JENNIR.

DON'T DO ANYTHING *"UNBALANCED"* BEFORE WE MEET AGAIN.

LET HER THINK THAT HE'S UNBALANCED. PERHAPS HE IS.

THERE ARE CERTAINLY MANY REASONS WHY HE SHOULD HAVE REFUSED THIS JOB HE HAS ACCEPTED SO PRECIPITOUSLY.

BUT, THOUGH THE FUTURE IS UNCERTAIN, JENNIR FEELS THAT FOR THE FIRST TIME IN A LONG TIME HE IS ON HIS WAY TO HAVING HIS TRUE BALANCE RESTORED.

CORUSCANT.

FIFTY DAYS HAVE PASSED SINCE HE LAST WALKED THESE CORRIDORS...

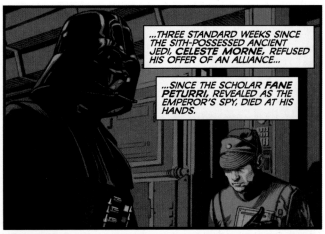

...THREE STANDARD WEEKS SINCE THE SITH-POSSESSED ANCIENT JEDI, *CELESTE MORNE*, REFUSED HIS OFFER OF AN ALLIANCE...

...SINCE THE SCHOLAR *FANE PETURRI*, REVEALED AS THE EMPEROR'S SPY, DIED AT HIS HANDS.

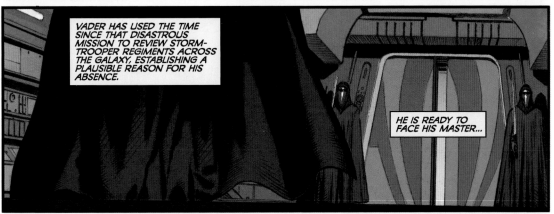

VADER HAS USED THE TIME SINCE THAT DISASTROUS MISSION TO REVIEW STORM-TROOPER REGIMENTS ACROSS THE GALAXY, ESTABLISHING A PLAUSIBLE REASON FOR HIS ABSENCE.

HE IS READY TO FACE HIS MASTER...

LORD VADER...YOU RETURN AT LAST.

WAS MY OLD FRIEND FANE PETURRI ABLE TO OBTAIN INFORMATION FROM THE PRISONER *JANKS* ABOUT THE ANTIQUITIES HE SEEKS?

I...I HAVE NOT HEARD FROM PETURRI SINCE WE PARTED COMPANY, MASTER.

OF COURSE, OF COURSE. RISE, APPRENTICE.

I AM CERTAIN YOU WERE MUCH MORE INTERESTED IN THE NEWS OF THE JEDI -- *DASS JENNIR* -- WHO HAD LATELY BEEN A MEMBER OF THE *UHUMELE'S* CREW...

A JEDI! NONE OF THE REPORTS THAT CAME HIS WAY MENTIONED A JEDI...

...HE HAD BEEN SO FOCUSED ON OBTAINING A WORKING SITH RELIC HE HAD NOT PURSUED ANY OTHER LINE OF QUESTIONING. IF HE HAS LET ANOTHER JEDI SLIP AWAY--

I HAVE WARNED YOU BEFORE ABOUT YOUR PREOCCUPATION WITH SURVIVING JEDI.

AND, SHOULD ANY JEDI ATTEMPT TO RAISE A HAND AGAINST US --

THE JEDI ORDER IS *BROKEN*, LORD VADER. YOU MUSTN'T EXPEND YOUR ENERGY CHASING RUMORS.

-- I HAVE ALREADY SET IN MOTION A PLAN TO DEAL WITH THEM.

A PLAN?

DOES THE PLAN INCLUDE HIM?

YOU ARE NEEDED ON *BANDOMEER*...

...THE IONITE MINERS THERE ARE REFUSING TO HONOR THEIR CONTRACTS WITH THE EMPIRE...

IT DOES NOT.

THE ARCHIPELAGO OF NOUA, TELERATH, IN THE INNER RIM.

TELERATH. AT ONE TIME IT WAS A MAJOR BANKING CENTER FOR MOST OF THE COLONIES AND THE INNER RIM. ITS SLOGAN WAS *"WHAT THE GALAXY FORGOT IT WANTED IN A BANK."*

AFTER THE *MANDALORIAN WARS,* IT WAS JUST FORGOTTEN.

LATELY, THERE HAS BEEN AN ATTEMPT TO TURN THE PLANET INTO A VACATION DESTINATION. DEFYING ALL GOOD SENSE, MANY SPECIES ENJOY WATER AND SAND--

CAN IT, *H2.* I DON'T NEED A HISTORY LESSON.

AS YOU COMMAND--

--MAN-WHO-KILLED-MY-MASTER.

SHUT UP.

WELCOME TO *NOUA,* THE GEM OF TELERATH! I SAW YOU COMING IN, AND I SAID TO MYSELF, FISH, THERE'S A FELLA WHO'S WANTING A RIDE.

YOU WON'T GET THIS KIND OF SERVICE FROM OTHER WATER TAXIS, NO SIR!

JUST A SHORT RIDE TO THE CITY CENTER, AND I WON'T EVEN CHARGE YOU FOR YOUR FLOATY DROID.

I EVEN ACCEPT THE NEW *IMPERIAL* CREDITS, CAP'N.

YOU KNOW, BACK IN THE DAY, TELERATH WAS ONE OF THE BIGGEST BANKING CENTERS FOR THE COLONIES AND THE INNER RIM...

...HAD A GOOD THING GOING FOR A SPELL -- LOTS OF TOURISTS. BUT THAT ALL GOT WASHED AWAY WHEN--

--THE GANGS MOVED IN.

"GANGS"? THERE'S MORE THAN ONE?

HEH. NOTHING GETS BY OL' FISH. I PICKED *YOU* OUT RIGHT AWAY. YOU'RE HERE FOR THE *TRYOUTS.*

'COURSE YOU ARE. NO OTHER *REASON* TO COME TO TELERATH ANYMORE. BUT I'M WARNING YOU, THE *SLAVERS* ARE A TOUGH CROWD -- ESPECIALLY THEIR HEAD ENFORCER, *DEMANNA.*

WHAT ABOUT THE *OTHER* GANG?

SPICE RUNNERS. →PHFFT←

RUN BY A COUPLE OF T'SURRI BROTHERS. IF ANYTHING, THE *SPICERS* ARE MORE DANGEROUS THAN THE SLAVERS -- WILDER, LESS ORGANIZED.

A SECOND GANG. WHY DIDN'T HIS EMPLOYER -- EMBER CHANKELI -- MENTION THE SPICERS?

DID HE ACCEPT THE JOB SHE OFFERED TOO READILY BECAUSE IT PRESENTED A CHANCE TO DEAL A BLOW TO THE SLAVE TRADE?

AFTER WHAT HAPPENED TO HIS FRIEND'S WIFE AND DAUGHTER, WAS HIS JUDGMENT CLOUDED BY EMOTION -- BY A DESIRE FOR VENGEANCE?

OR BY A DIFFERENT DESIRE ALTOGETHER?

'TWEEN THE TWO GANGS, THE TOWN HAS GONE TO BLAZES.

MAY THE SEA OR THE SEWER TAKE THE LOT OF 'EM.

NO OFFENSE.

THE SLAVERS ARE HOLDING THEIR TRYOUTS IN THE MAIN SQUARE -- AT THE TOP OF THAT RAMP.

HERE.

B-BUT THIS IS *TOO MUCH* FOR THE FARE!

CHINK!

CONSIDER YOURSELF ON RETAINER.

RETAINER? *YES, SIR!*

WHATEVER YOU SAY, CAP'N!

FISH IS AT YOUR SERVICE! AND PARDON MY EARLIER COMMENTS, SIR --

--I DIDN'T KNOW YOU WAS A *GENTLEMAN!*

THE OLD MAN'S WORDS ARE LOST IN THE CLASH OF STEEL AND THE FLOOD OF SENSATIONS EMANATING FROM THE CROWD.

EXCITEMENT... DESPERATION... FEAR.

EXCEPT FOR THE BIG CHAGRIAN IN THE RING. HE PROJECTS AN ALMOST JEDI-LIKE CALM.

DASS JENNIR REACHES OUT WITH HIS SENSES. THE CHAGRIAN HAS NO CONNECTION TO THE FORCE...

...BUT IN THE CROWD, A DOZEN SMALL DETAILS CRY OUT TO BE NOTICED.

34

SWORDS CARRIED IN ADDITION TO -- OR EVEN INSTEAD OF -- BLASTERS...

...THE PALPABLE ANGUISH IN ONE BOY AS HIS PRIDE COLLIDES WITH FEAR FOR HIS LIFE...

...AND THE FACE OF HIS EMPLOYER --

-- WHO TOLD HIM ONLY *HALF* THE TRUTH.

BUT IT IS THE FIGHT -- IF SUCH A ONE-SIDED CONTEST CAN BE CALLED A "FIGHT" -- THAT HOLDS THE CROWD'S ATTENTION.

UNWORTHY.

AND DEMANNA PUTS ANOTHER ONE IN THE DUST!

HEY, YOU GONNA FIGHT? YOU GOTTA SIGN UP FIRST...AND DON'T THINK ABOUT JUMPING AHEAD OF *ME*-- I'M NEXT!

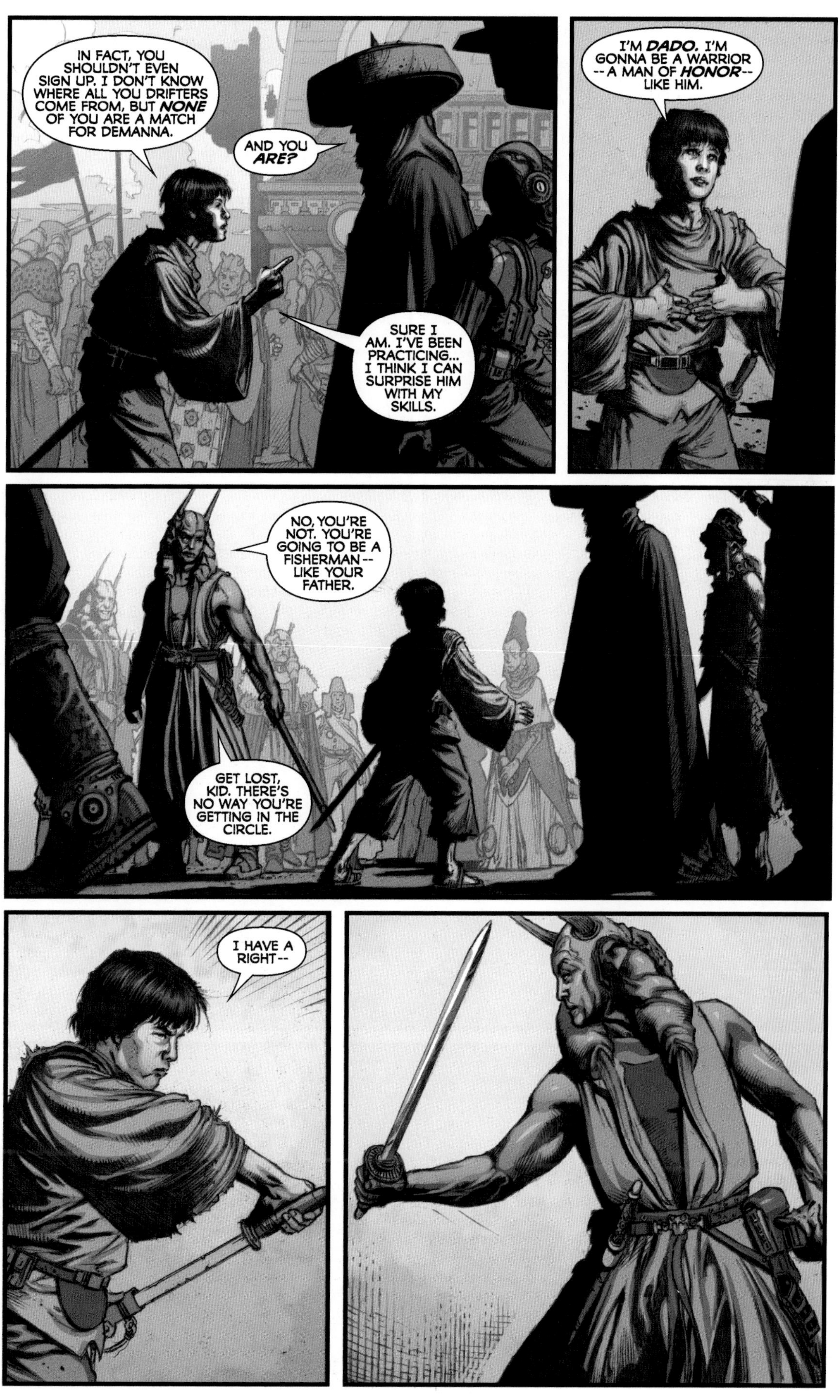

IN FACT, YOU SHOULDN'T EVEN SIGN UP. I DON'T KNOW WHERE ALL YOU DRIFTERS COME FROM, BUT NONE OF YOU ARE A MATCH FOR DEMANNA.
AND YOU ARE?
SURE I AM. I'VE BEEN PRACTICING... I THINK I CAN SURPRISE HIM WITH MY SKILLS.
I'M DADO. I'M GONNA BE A WARRIOR --A MAN OF HONOR-- LIKE HIM.
NO, YOU'RE NOT. YOU'RE GOING TO BE A FISHERMAN-- LIKE YOUR FATHER.
GET LOST, KID. THERE'S NO WAY YOU'RE GETTING IN THE CIRCLE.
I HAVE A RIGHT--

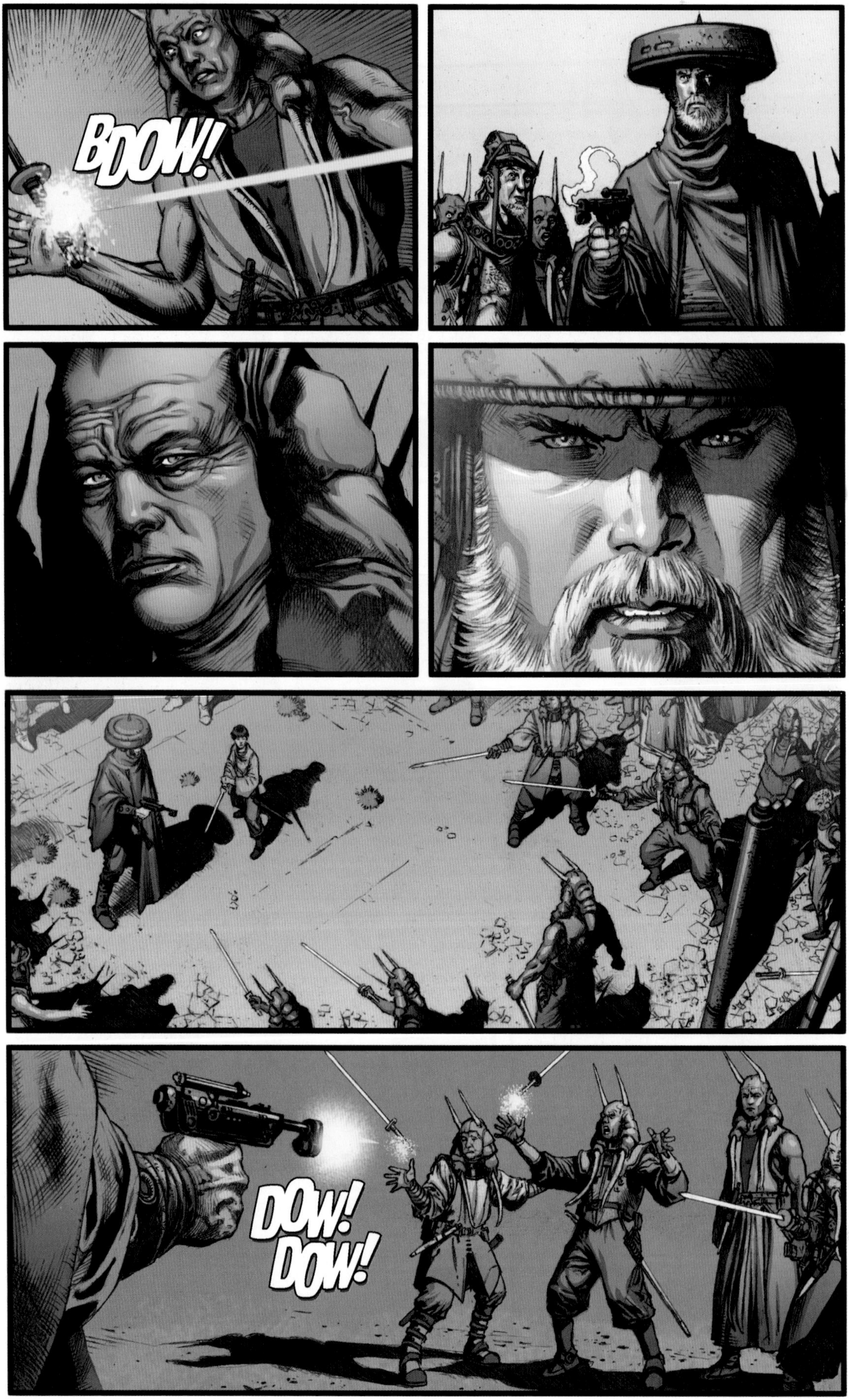
BDOW!
DOW!
DOW!

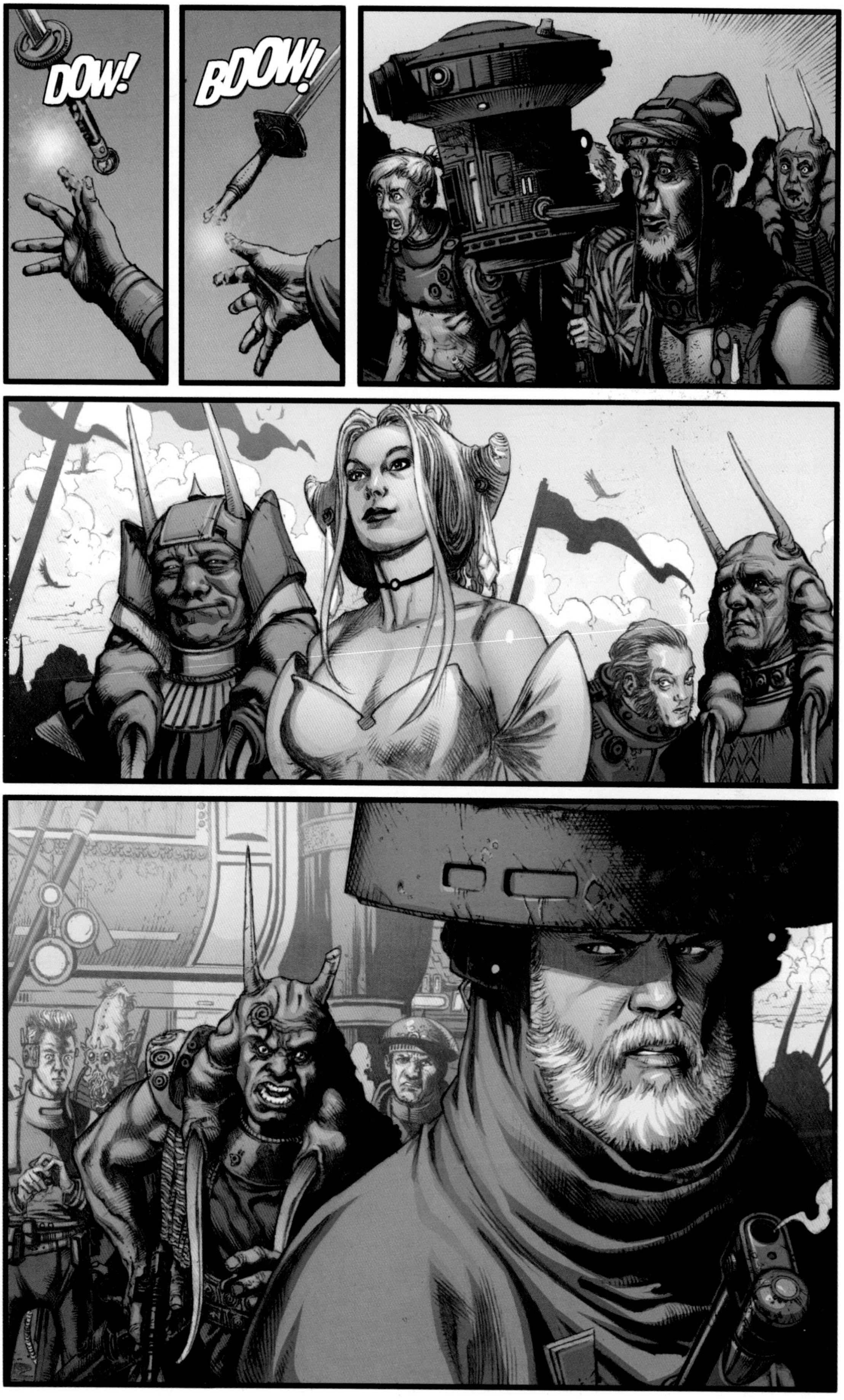
DOW!
BDOW!

STOP!

BDEW!

NO BLASTERS!

REMEMBER *SWORD LAW!*

"SWORD LAW"?

IT IS THE LAW ON TELERATH. ALL DISPUTES MUST BE SETTLED WITH THE BLADE -- A WARRIOR STANDS OR FALLS BY THE STRENGTH OF HIS OWN RIGHT ARM.

BY HOLDING TO THIS LAW--

--PEACE IS PRESERVED, AS WELL AS HONOR.

TO RESORT TO A BLASTER IS TO BREAK THE PEACE, TO ENDANGER CIVILIANS, AND TO RELINQUISH ALL CLAIM TO HONOR.

YOU, STRANGER, COULD NOT HAVE KNOWN OF THIS LAW, AND ARE THEREFORE NOT GUILTY OF BREAKING IT. BUT YOU HAVE BEEN WARNED. ANY FUTURE INFRACTION WILL BE MET WITH DECISIVE ACTION.

BUT YOU, *YOU* HAVE NO CLAIM TO IGNORANCE OF THE LAW -- NOR TO HONOR!

BY ATTEMPTING TO SHOOT THIS MAN IN THE BACK, YOU HAVE BROUGHT SHAME TO YOURSELF AND OUR ORGANIZATION!

BUT, DEMANNA, I WAS ONLY TRYING TO--!

LET THIS BE A LESSON TO ALL WHO WOULD DISHONOR THE LAW!

HUK!

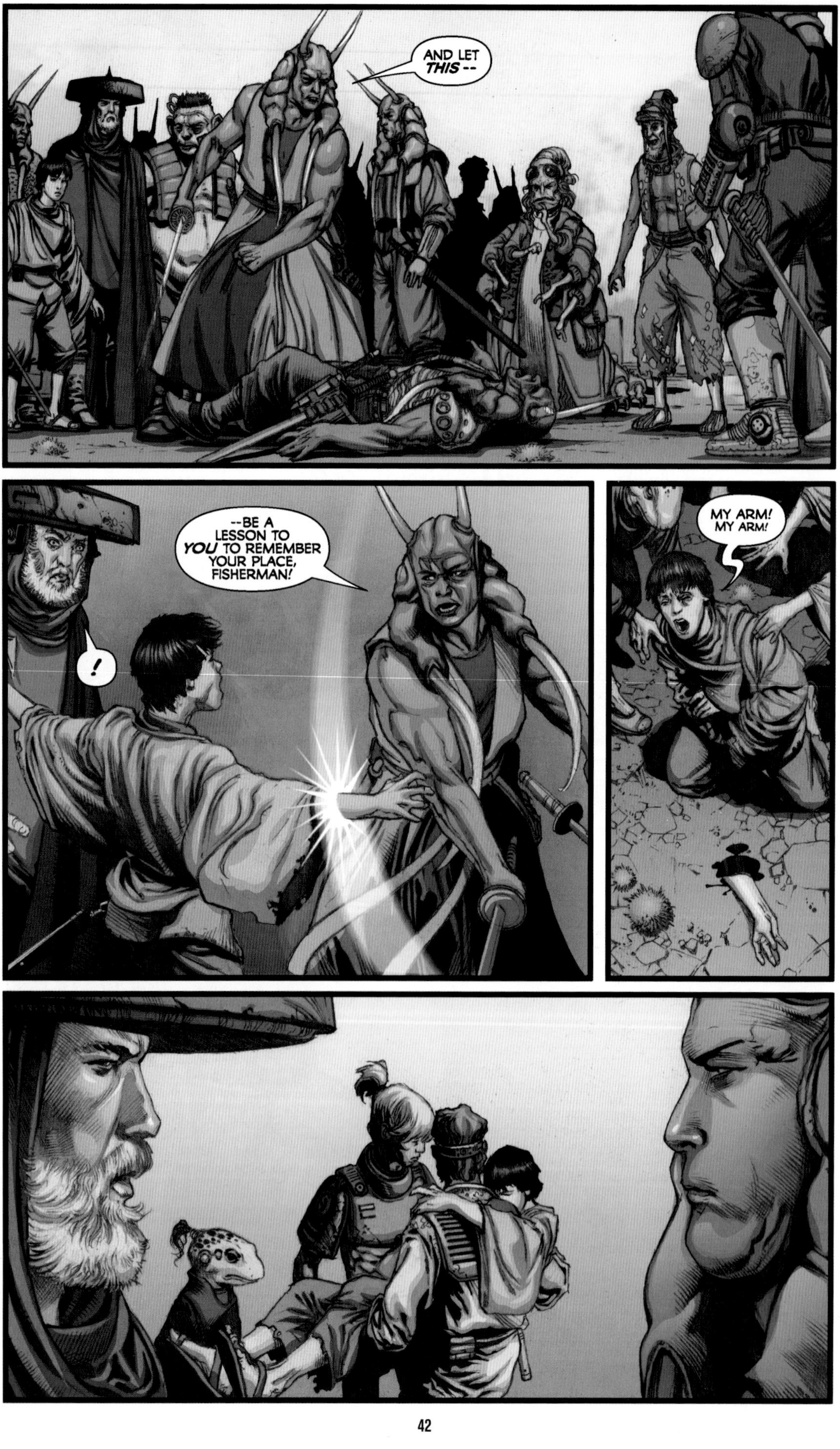
AND LET THIS --
--BE A LESSON TO YOU TO REMEMBER YOUR PLACE, FISHERMAN!
!
MY ARM! MY ARM!

ENOUGH. THE TRYOUTS ARE OVER!

EVERYONE BACK TO THE HOUSE!

THE STRANGER IS AMAZING! I'VE *NEVER* SEEN SHOOTING LIKE THAT!

IMPRESSIVE. YOU'VE DEFINITELY ATTRACTED DEMANNA'S INTEREST.

COME BY MY PLACE LATER...

...EVERYTHING'S GOING AS PLANNED.

IS IT? JENNIR'S NOT SURE.

BUT WHAT HAD HE EXPECTED?

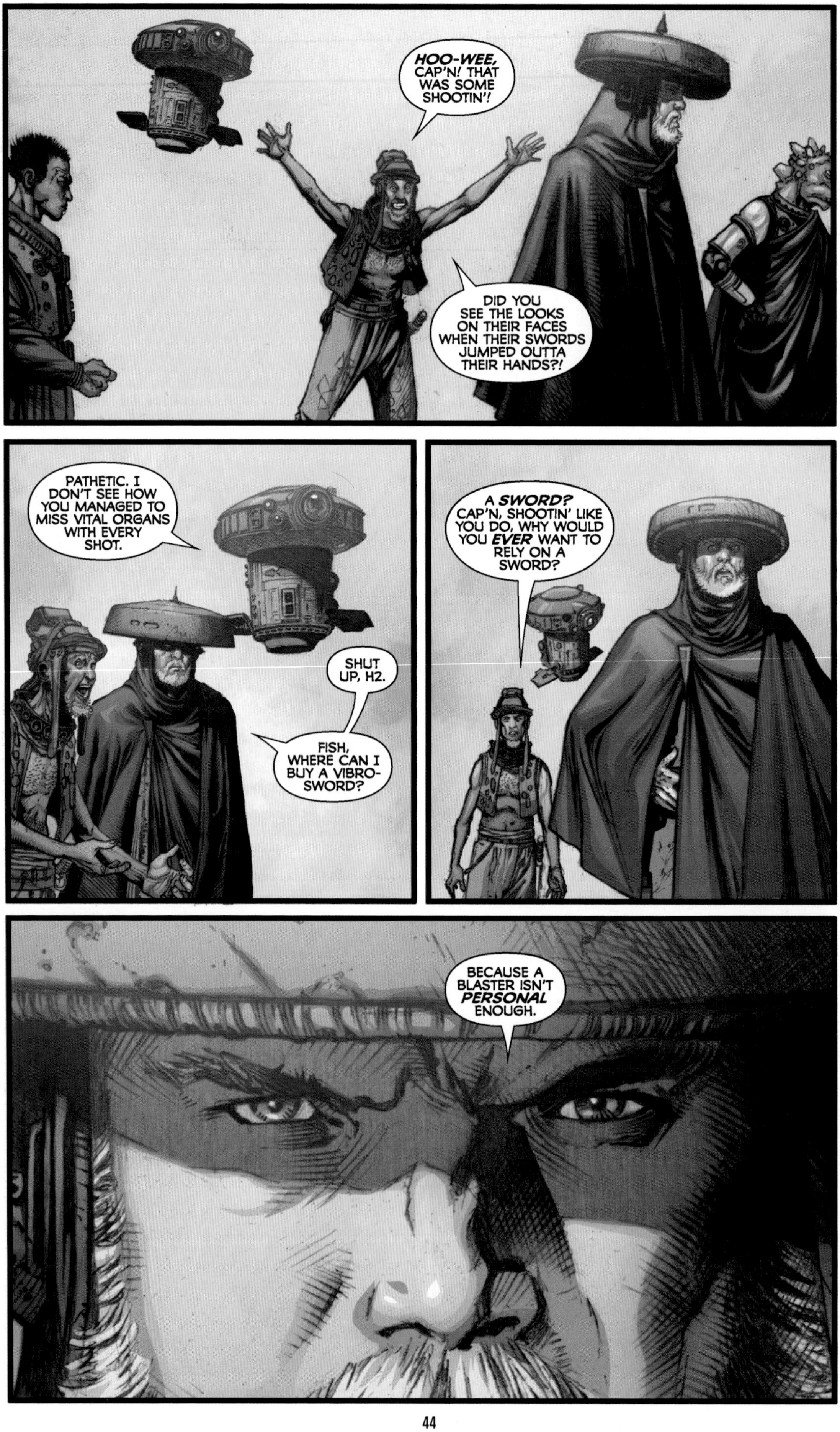
HOO-WEE, CAP'N! THAT WAS SOME SHOOTIN'!
DID YOU SEE THE LOOKS ON THEIR FACES WHEN THEIR SWORDS JUMPED OUTTA THEIR HANDS?!
PATHETIC. I DON'T SEE HOW YOU MANAGED TO MISS VITAL ORGANS WITH EVERY SHOT.
SHUT UP, H2.
FISH, WHERE CAN I BUY A VIBRO-SWORD?
A SWORD? CAP'N, SHOOTIN' LIKE YOU DO, WHY WOULD YOU EVER WANT TO RELY ON A SWORD?
BECAUSE A BLASTER ISN'T PERSONAL ENOUGH.

BANDOMEER, IN THE OUTER RIM.

WHY HAS HIS MASTER SENT HIM HERE?

WHY, WHEN HE HAS INFORMATION ABOUT A SURVIVING JEDI, WOULD HIS MASTER SEND HIM AWAY?

ANY COMPETENT COMMANDER COULD OVERSEE THIS MISSION. THE MINERS ARE LIGHTLY ARMED, BARELY A THREAT.

IS IT POSSIBLE THAT HIS MASTER KNOWS OF HIS FAILED ATTEMPT TO ENLIST CELESTE MORNE AS AN APPRENTICE?

COULD HE KNOW OF FANE PETURRI'S FATE?

IS THIS MISSION A MOVE TO GET HIM OUT OF THE WAY SO THAT HE DOESN'T DISCOVER THE EMPEROR'S PLAN FOR DEALING WITH THE SURVIVING JEDI?

OR COULD IT BE A MOVE TO JUST GET HIM OUT OF THE WAY -- PERMANENTLY?

VADER KNOWS HIS MASTER'S EYES ARE UPON HIM.

BUT WHETHER THEY VIEW HIM WITH SUSPICION OR FAVOR, HE CANNOT TELL.

HE MUST PUT THOSE SUSPICIONS AWAY.

HIS MASTER WOULD NOT SEND HIM HERE IF HE WAS NOT NEEDED.

THEN WHY SO MANY DOUBTS?

WHY, WHEN HIS PRESENT COURSE IS SO CLEAR, ARE THERE SO MANY QUESTIONS FROM THE RECENT PAST?

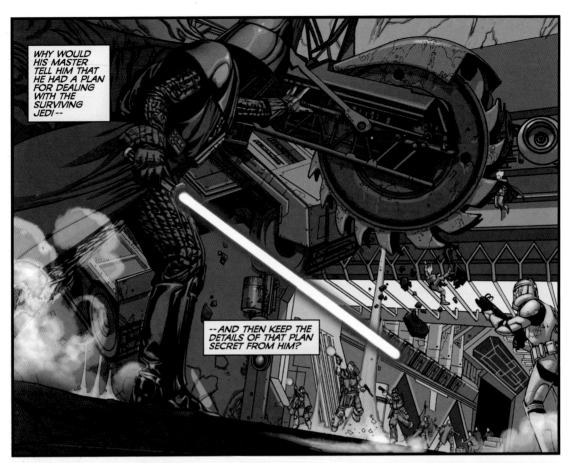

WHY WOULD HIS MASTER TELL HIM THAT HE HAD A PLAN FOR DEALING WITH THE SURVIVING JEDI--

--AND THEN KEEP THE DETAILS OF THAT PLAN SECRET FROM HIM?

UNLESS THERE IS SUSPICION IN HIS MASTER'S MIND...

...SUSPICION FED BY VADER'S OWN BADLY CONCEALED GUILT? PERHAPS.

IF HE *HAD* HIS MASTER'S TRUST, WHY DIDN'T THE EMPEROR INFORM HIM THAT THE PRISONER JANKS HAD CREWED A SMUGGLING VESSEL WITH A JEDI?

WHY WOULDN'T HIS MASTER TELL HIM ABOUT THIS...

THAT SWORDSMITH WAS IMPRESSED WHEN YOU PICKED OUT THAT OLD RELIC.

IF YOU KNOW YOUR WAY WITH A SWORD LIKE YOU DO A BLASTER...

YOU'LL BE NEEDIN' A PLACE TO STAY, CAP'N. YOU JUST FOLLOW ME -- OL' FISH WILL TAKE YOU TO THE FINEST PLACE IN TOWN.

THAT'S ALL RIGHT. I'LL STAY HERE.

EMBER'S FIRE? BUT, THAT PLACE IS --

OH. SURE THING, CAP'N. I GET IT.

IF YOU NEED ME, I'LL BE AS CLOSE AS A SHOUT.

C'MERE, HONEY.

I SAID, C'MERE!

LET GO! NOT TODAY! YOU KNOW WHAT HAPPENED HERE.

I KNOW WHAT MY CREDITS BUY HERE!

NOT TODAY! TAM--!

KL!CK!

WHA--?!
AAAAH--!

SPLOOSH!!

HEH-HEH! SOME THINGS NEVER CHANGE.

TAM! SYLVA! WHAT DID I TELL YOU ABOUT DOING THAT TO PAYING CUSTOMERS?!

THAT'S COMING OUT OF YOUR--

--OH. UH, GOOD AFTERNOON... I, UH...

ARE YOU THE PROPRIETOR?

EMBER CHANKELI, AT YOUR SERVICE.

I'D LIKE TO SEE ABOUT A ROOM...

CERTAINLY. FOLLOW ME AND I'LL GET YOU SET UP.

TAM! CLEAN THE BLOOD OFF THESE STEPS!

PAY NO ATTENTION TO IT. THE SON OF ONE OF MY GIRLS HAD AN ACCIDENT.

WE DON'T ALLOW ANY VIOLENCE HERE.

THE BOY -- *DADO* -- FROM THE FIGHT?

I *SUPPOSE* THAT'S HIS NAME -- THE LITTLE IDIOT. WHAT WAS HE THINKING, DRAWING A SWORD AGAINST MORS DEMANNA?

NOW YOU'VE GOTTEN A FIRSTHAND LOOK AT WHAT WE'RE UP AGAINST HERE...

...THOSE *SLAVERS* ARE RUINING MY BUSINESS.

BUT I THINK YOU MANAGED TO PIQUE THEIR INTEREST WITH YOUR FANCY SHOOTING.

I'M SURE YOU'LL BE ACCEPTED INTO THE GANG--

--AS SOON AS THEY GET OVER WANTING TO *KILL* YOU. EVEN THOUGH IT WAS DEMANNA THAT KILLED HIM, I THINK THEY BLAME *YOU* FOR THE DEATH OF THEIR FRIEND.

DON'T WORRY. THIS PLACE IS NEUTRAL TERRITORY--THEY WON'T ATTACK YOU HERE. BUT I'D WAIT A FEW DAYS BEFORE GOING OUTSIDE.

DEMANNA WILL BRING THEM AROUND. HE'LL WANT YOU AS AN ASSET RATHER THAN AN ENEMY. YOU'LL SEE.

WHAT ABOUT THE *SPICE RUNNERS?*

THE SPICE RUN--? OH, THEM. WELL--

--THEY'RE NOT A PROBLEM. THE SLAVERS PREY ON EVERY NEWCOMER, RUINING THE TOURIST TRADE.

THE SPICERS JUST USE NOUA AS THEIR HEADQUARTERS. ALL OF THE SPICE STAYS AT THEIR REFINERY... ON THE SECOND MOON.

YOU DON'T HAVE TO WORRY ABOUT THEM. *JUST* THE SLAVERS.

BUT REMEMBER, NO ONE CAN KNOW THAT I HIRED YOU. *HOWEVER* YOU GET THE JOB DONE -- WHATEVER YOU HAVE TO DO TO *GET RID* OF THE SLAVERS -- IT'S ALL ON YOU. THAT WAS OUR DEAL.

I HAVEN'T FORGOTTEN. I INTEND TO KEEP MY END OF THE BARGAIN -- AS LONG AS YOU KEEP YOURS.

HERE'S HALF YOUR PAYMENT. YOU GET THE REST WHEN THE JOB'S FINISHED. I PUT YOU IN ROOM FOUR -- DOWN THE HALL.

DON'T FORGET WHAT I SAID -- YOU NEED TO LAY LOW FOR A DAY OR SO. STAY IN YOUR ROOM.

I'D COUNT THE MONEY, IF I WERE YOU.

JUST SAYING.

SIR...?

THANK YOU, SIR! THEY SAID YOU'RE THE ONE WHO SAVED MY BOY'S LIFE. I OWE YOU MORE THAN --

THE BOY FROM THE SQUARE? *DADO?*

YES. I'M NIKOLLANE, HIS MOTHER.

IS HE ALL RIGHT?

WE STOPPED THE BLEEDING...AND -- MONA GAVE HIM SOMETHING...

IT WILL ALLOW HIM TO SLEEP, BUT THAT'S ABOUT ALL.

HE NEEDS A MEDICO, BUT ALL OF THEM LEFT -- ALONG WITH EVERYONE ELSE WHO COULD AFFORD A TICKET OFF-WORLD.

LET ME SEE WHAT *I* CAN DO.

YOU'RE A DOCTOR? BUT EVERYBODY SAID YOU WERE A... WARRIOR...

I'M *NOT* A DOCTOR -- BUT I'VE SEEN MANY WOUNDS LIKE DADO'S.

CLICK

HIS PAIN
SHOULD BE
LESS NOW.

THANK
YOU, SIR --

DASS
JENNIR.

THANK
YOU, DASS
JENNIR.

YOU CAN'T STAY OUT OF OTHER PEOPLE'S BUSINESS, CAN YOU? FIRST IT WAS THAT ANGRY NOSAURIAN, NOW IT'S THIS KID.

DID YOU HEAR ME, MAN-WHO-KILLED-MY-MASTER? I SAID --

GO TO THE SHIP. GET IT READY FOR DEPARTURE.

LEAVING ALREADY?

IT WILL BE A SHORT TRIP. AND FIND THE OLD MAN, FISH. TELL HIM THAT I'LL NEED HIM AND HIS BOAT AS SOON AS IT'S DARK.

BUT THE LADY SAID YOU SHOULD STAY IN -- THE SLAVERS ARE WAITING FOR YOU.

I KNOW --

"-- I'M BEGINNING TO THINK THAT MAY BE THE FIRST TRUE THING SHE HAS SAID TO ME."

DON'T WORRY, *KEN-KIBA.* EVERYTHING IS GOING ACCORDING TO PLAN.

AND YOU'RE SURE THIS MAN YOU HIRED CAN DO WHAT WE NEED HIM TO DO, EMBER?

HE'S THE PERFECT CANDIDATE. I HAD ANTICIPATED HAVING TO HIRE *SEVERAL* WARRIORS, BUT HE BESTED THE THUGS I'D HIRED ON CATO NEIMOIDIA WITH EASE. HE'S A GREAT FIGHTER, BUT EASILY MANIPULATED.

RELAX, KEN-KIBA, AND ENJOY THE GIFT I HAVE BROUGHT YOU. IS SHE NOT EVERYTHING YOU SAID YOU DESIRED?

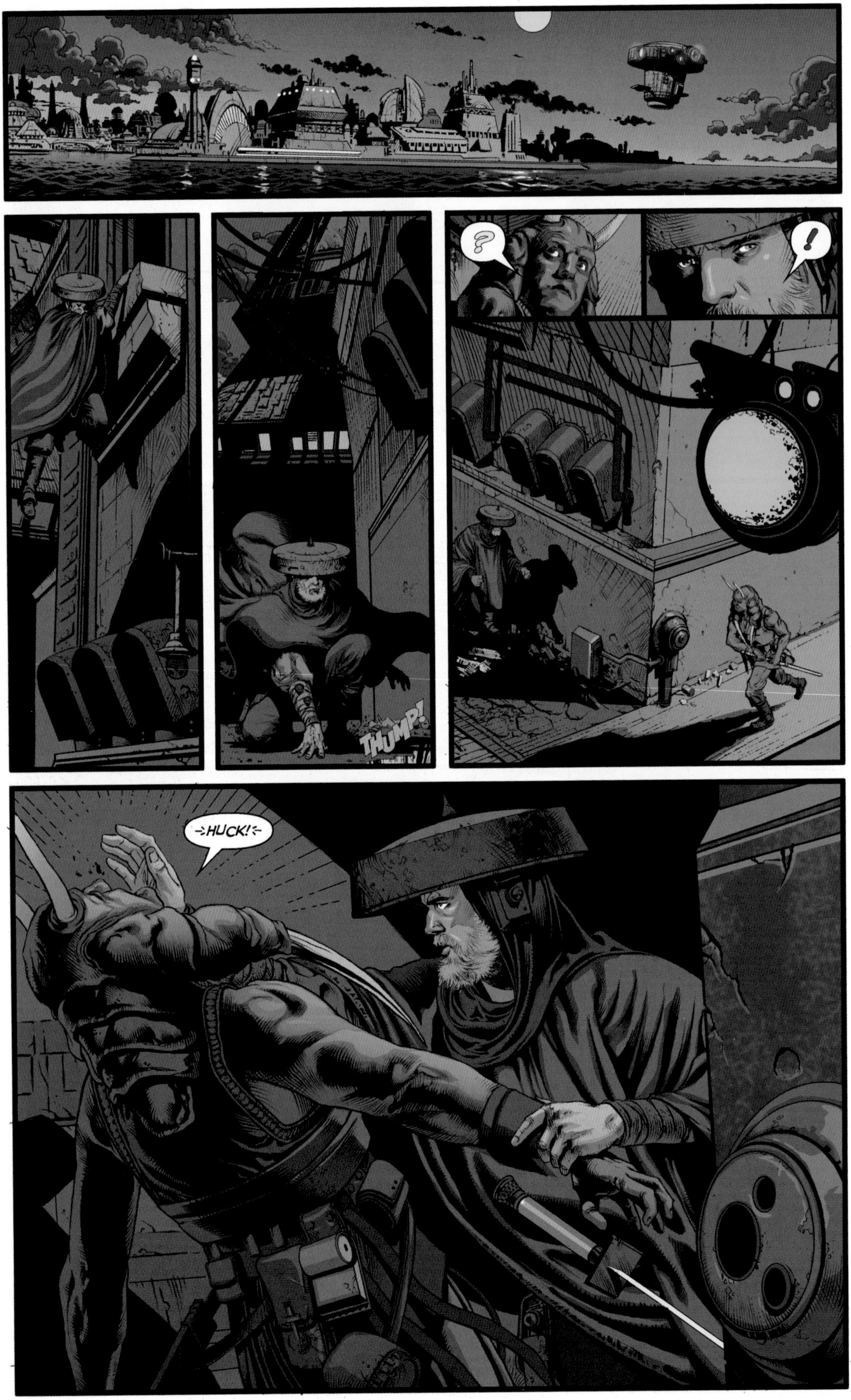
?
!
THUMP!
HUCK!

THE SLAVERS **ARE** LYING IN WAIT FOR HIM. ONLY THE **FORCE** ALERTED HIM TO THE CHAGRIAN'S PRESENCE.

ARMED WITH HIS CONNECTION TO THE FORCE, JENNIR MIGHT NEED NO OTHER WEAPONS. BUT HERE IS ONE THAT MAY PROVE VALUABLE -- THE KNIFE THAT ALL OF THE SLAVERS CARRY AS A SIGN OF THEIR AFFILIATION...

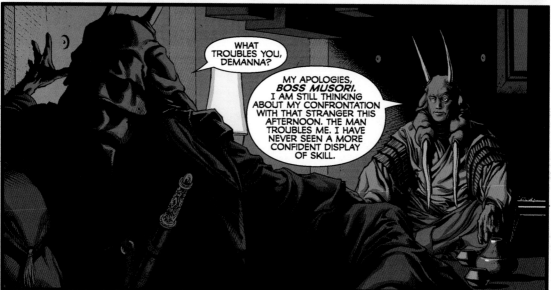

WHAT TROUBLES YOU, DEMANNA?

MY APOLOGIES, **BOSS MUSORI.** I AM STILL THINKING ABOUT MY CONFRONTATION WITH THAT STRANGER THIS AFTERNOON. THE MAN TROUBLES ME. I HAVE NEVER SEEN A MORE CONFIDENT DISPLAY OF SKILL.

WORSE, I DO NOT CARE FOR THE WAY THE MEN ARE QUESTIONING MY DECISION TO LET THE MAN LIVE.

PUT IT FROM YOUR MIND. YOU MADE THE RIGHT DECISION -- AND I HAVE NO DOUBT YOU ARE THE BETTER OF ANY WARRIOR IN THE SECTOR.

STILL, IF THE MAN IS AS IMPRESSIVE AS YOU SAY, THEN NO MATTER WHAT THE RANK AND FILE THINK, HE SHOULD BE WORKING FOR US...

FISH, WAIT HERE. I'LL BE BACK BY MORNING.

YOU GOT IT, BOSS.

"...AND IF HE REFUSES, YOU CAN REDEEM YOURSELF BY KILLING HIM."

HURRY IT UP, YOU WORTHLESS SKUGS!

HEY, *KEN-GIREE!* TAKE A LOOK--

--THERE'S A SHIP COMIN' IN!

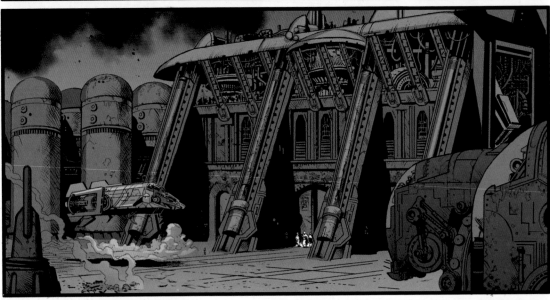

THIS IS A *PRIVATE* OPERATION. WE DON'T ALLOW VISITORS, STRANGER.

I MEAN NO DISRESPECT, BUT MY ASTROMECH DROID REQUIRES RECALIBRATION. I WAS HOPING I COULD USE DATA FROM ONE OF YOURS TO MAKE THE NECESSARY ADJUSTMENTS.

OH, SURE. BLAME IT ON ME!

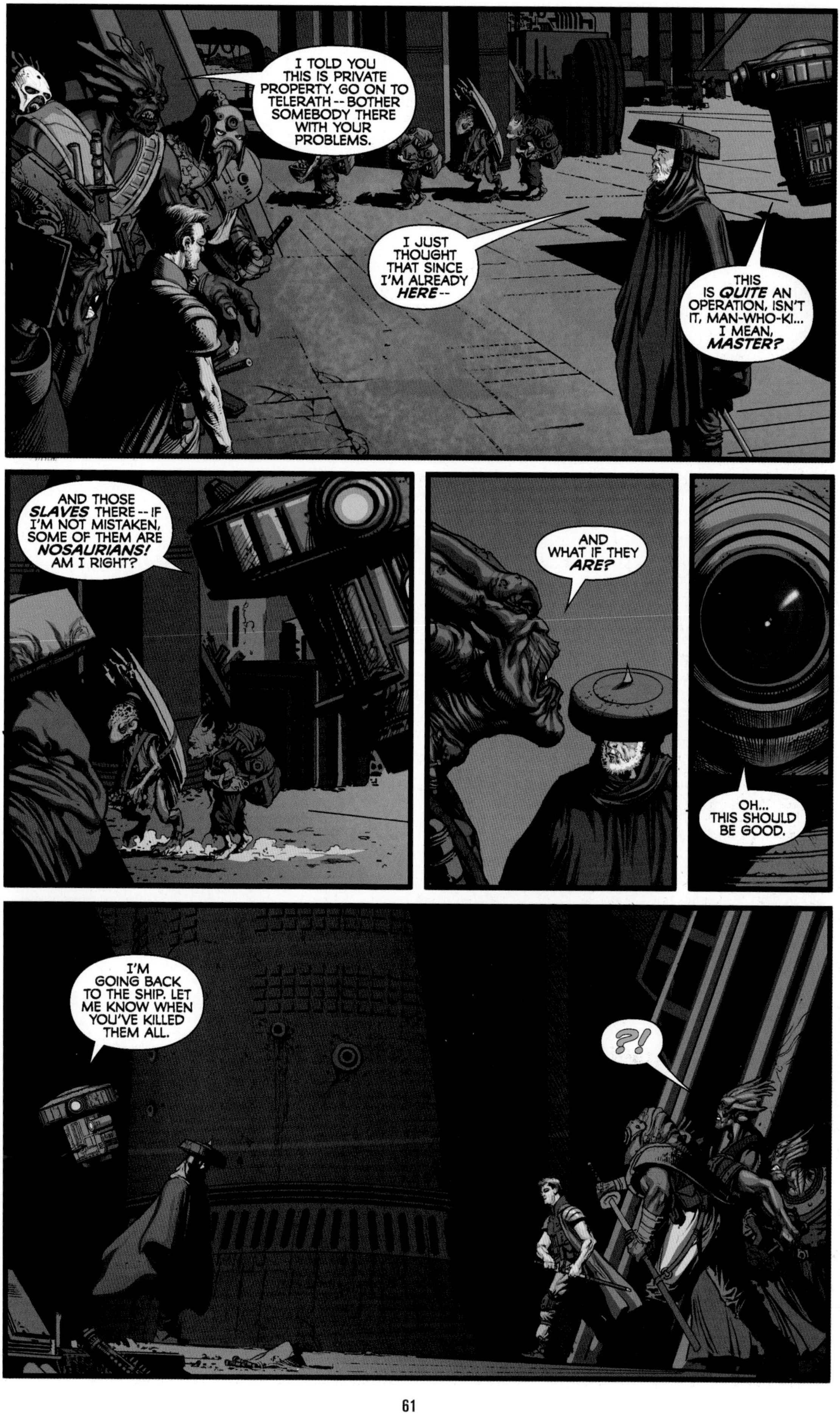
I TOLD YOU THIS IS PRIVATE PROPERTY. GO ON TO TELERATH -- BOTHER SOMEBODY THERE WITH YOUR PROBLEMS.
I JUST THOUGHT THAT SINCE I'M ALREADY *HERE* --
THIS IS *QUITE* AN OPERATION, ISN'T IT, MAN-WHO-KI... I MEAN, *MASTER?*
AND THOSE *SLAVES* THERE -- IF I'M NOT MISTAKEN, SOME OF THEM ARE *NOSAURIANS!* AM I RIGHT?
AND WHAT IF THEY *ARE?*
OH... THIS SHOULD BE GOOD.
I'M GOING BACK TO THE SHIP. LET ME KNOW WHEN YOU'VE KILLED THEM ALL.
?!

HE'S GOT A BLASTER!

IT'S NOT A FAIR FIGHT. IT WAS NEVER MEANT TO BE.

THIS ISN'T ABOUT A MARTIAL CHALLENGE --

CURSE THE "SWORD LAW"! FALL BACK!

-- IT'S ABOUT REMOVING AN EVIL FROM THE GALAXY.

AS A JEDI, JENNIR WAS A PEACEKEEPER -- PROTECTING THE INNOCENT -- SUPPORTING THE LAWS OF THE REPUBLIC...

HOLD HIM OFF WHILE WE GET ABOVE HIM!

...BUT, WITHOUT LAWS -- WITHOUT THE REPUBLIC --

-- HE WILL BECOME A PEACEMAKER...

AIIIIEEE!

...REMOVING THOSE WHO WOULD HARM THE DEFENSELESS.

WHERE ARE OUR BLASTED BLASTERS?!

I THINK WE LEFT 'EM ON THE SHIP, 'GIREE...

WHA--?!

HOW'D HE GET UP HERE?

THE FORCE IS A POWERFUL ALLY.

THE "FORCE"?

GENERAL JENNIR!

HE'S A JEDI!

GENERAL, *EH?* SO, YOU *KNOW* THESE SKUGS? YOU *CARE* FOR THEM?

TOO BAD FOR YOU -- AND THEM.

SEE, THE WAR'S OVER, GENERAL, AND *YOU LOST* --

--JUST LIKE YOU'VE LOST NOW.

THIS IS WHAT'S GOING TO HAPPEN -- YOU'RE GOING TO HAND OVER YOUR BLASTER, OR I'M GOING TO SEPARATE THIS OLD GIRL FROM WHAT'S LEFT OF HER SORRY LIFE.

IT SEEMS YOU LEAVE ME NO CHOICE.

I DON'T.

VERY WELL. *CATCH!*

!

?

REMEMBER WHAT I SAID ABOUT THE FORCE?

YOU CAME BACK FOR US.

YOU'VE SAVED US, JUST AS I FORETOLD.

I KNEW YOU WOULD. I TOLD THE OTHERS. I SAID, *THERE AREN'T MANY THINGS YOU CAN COUNT ON IN THIS LIFE, BUT A JEDI IS ONE OF THEM!*

UH, YES...

GENERAL JENNIR RETURNED!

WE'RE FREE!

BLESS YOU, GENERAL!

LISTEN, YOU MUST GO. IT'S TIME FOR YOU TO LEAVE.

BUT WHERE? WHERE CAN WE GO?

WHEREVER YOU WANT-- SOMEPLACE SAFE. TAKE THOSE SHIPS. MAKE NEW LIVES FOR YOURSELVES...

"...FAR AWAY FROM HERE."

"WHAT ABOUT *YOU,* GENERAL?"

"I STILL HAVE WORK TO DO..."

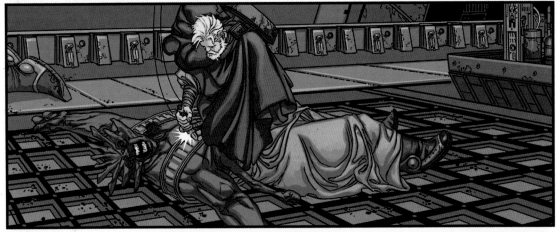

"...I HAVE TO LEAVE THE SPICE-RUNNERS A MESSAGE."

BANDOMEER.

THE MINERS HAVE SURRENDERED, MY LORD. THE LAST SURVIVORS ARE BEING ROUNDED UP.

I HAVE OUR CASUALTY REPORTS--

--FOURTEEN DEAD, TWENTY-THREE WOUND--

COMMANDER VILL, I HAVE A QUESTION. I REQUIRE A *TRUTHFUL* ANSWER.

UH, OF COURSE, SIR.

THE EMPEROR FORESAW THAT THE JEDI WOULD ATTEMPT TO THWART HIS MOVE TO CONSOLIDATE THE REPUBLIC INTO AN EMPIRE. HE PREPARED YOU -- PREPARED *ALL* OF THE CLONES -- BY *INDOCTRINATING* YOU WITH INSTRUCTIONS FOR *ORDER 66...*

...

YES, SIR?

HAVE YOU BEEN INDOCTRINATED WITH A SIMILAR ORDER TO ATTACK *ME* IF THE EMPEROR SO COMMANDS?

UH, SIR...EVEN IF THERE *WERE* SUCH AN ORDER, I DO NOT HAVE THE AUTHORITY TO DIVULGE...

VILL'S ANSWER IS AS GOOD AS A CONFIRMATION.

~GAK!~

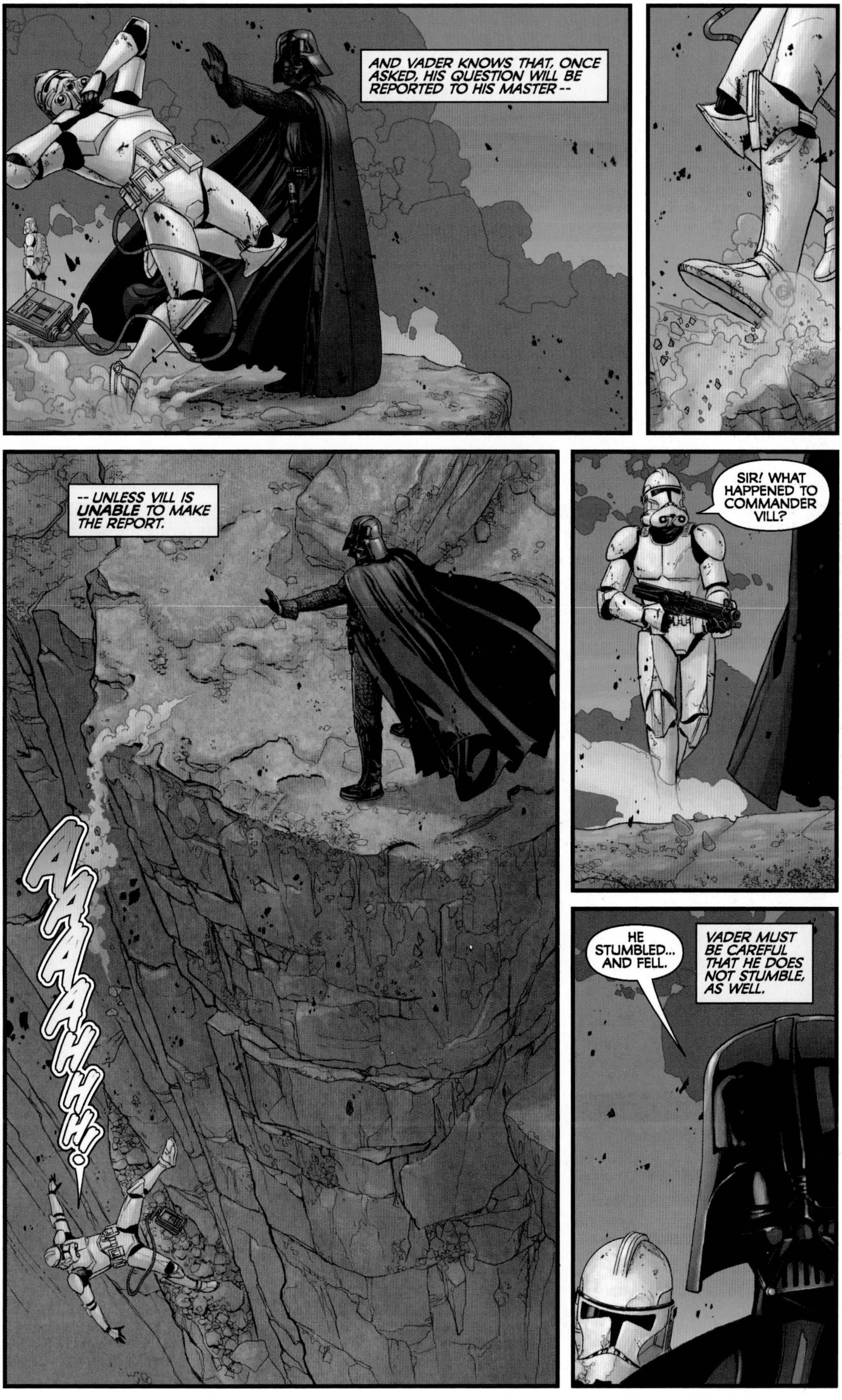
AND VADER KNOWS THAT, ONCE ASKED, HIS QUESTION WILL BE REPORTED TO HIS MASTER --
-- UNLESS VILL IS UNABLE TO MAKE THE REPORT.
AAAAAHHHH!
SIR! WHAT HAPPENED TO COMMANDER VILL?
HE STUMBLED... AND FELL.
VADER MUST BE CAREFUL THAT HE DOES NOT STUMBLE, AS WELL.

THAT TRIP TOOK LONGER THAN I'D PLANNED.

DROP ME AT THE RAMP TO THE MAIN SQUARE, FISH--

"-- THERE'S TOO MUCH DAYLIGHT TO RISK CLIMBING BACK INTO MY ROOM AT THE INN."

HAS OUR GUEST HAD HIS BREAKFAST YET?

HE WASN'T IN HIS ROOM WHEN I WENT TO TAKE HIS ORDER, MISTRESS. HIS BED HAD NOT BEEN SLEPT IN.

THE OVERT TENSION OF THE DAY BEFORE HAS PASSED --

-- BUT ONE ASPECT REMAINS. JENNIR SENSES A FAMILIAR STILLNESS...

KEEP QUIET, H2.

WHAT DID I DO TO WARRANT THAT? I HAVEN'T SAID A WORD SINCE YOU KILLED THOSE --

OH.

MORS DEMANNA. A FINE MORNING.

THAT IT IS.

I WAS *LOOKING* FOR YOU, *STRANGER.*

THE NAME'S DASS JENNIR. I WAS HOPING TO FIND *YOU,* AS WELL.

WHERE DID HE *GO?!* DID *YOU* SEE HIM LEAVE?

I'M SORRY, MISTRESS...

...I WAS WITH MY INJURED SON ALL NIGHT --

I DON'T CARE ABOUT YOUR SON! IF DASS JENNIR WENT *OUTSIDE* -- IF HE WAS *KILLED* BY THOSE SLAVERS --

--I'LL HAVE YOU ALL...

?

THIS IS GOING BETTER THAN I'D HOPED.

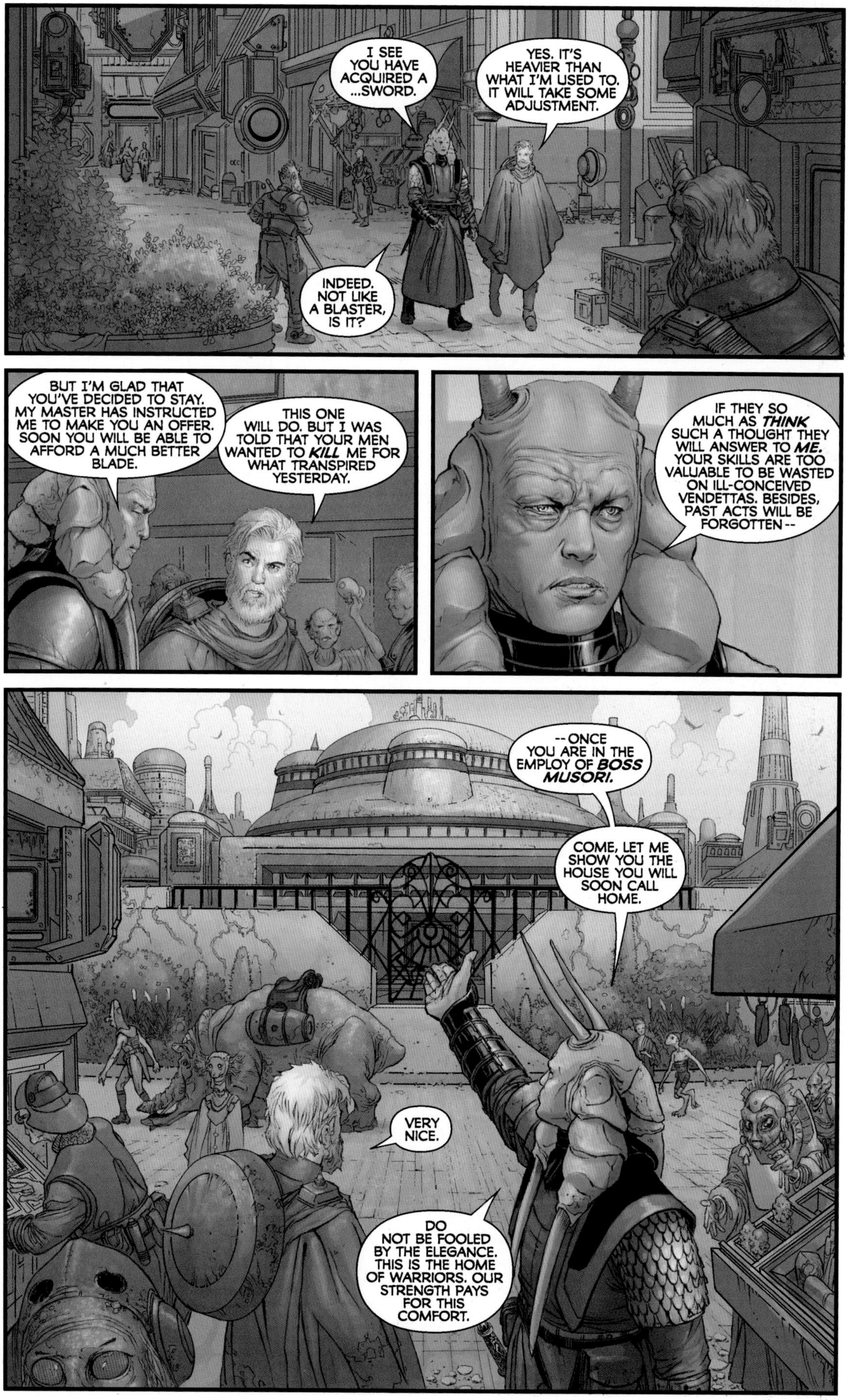
I SEE YOU HAVE ACQUIRED A ...SWORD.
YES. IT'S HEAVIER THAN WHAT I'M USED TO. IT WILL TAKE SOME ADJUSTMENT.
INDEED. NOT LIKE A BLASTER, IS IT?
BUT I'M GLAD THAT YOU'VE DECIDED TO STAY. MY MASTER HAS INSTRUCTED ME TO MAKE YOU AN OFFER. SOON YOU WILL BE ABLE TO AFFORD A MUCH BETTER BLADE.
THIS ONE WILL DO. BUT I WAS TOLD THAT YOUR MEN WANTED TO *KILL* ME FOR WHAT TRANSPIRED YESTERDAY.
IF THEY SO MUCH AS *THINK* SUCH A THOUGHT THEY WILL ANSWER TO *ME.* YOUR SKILLS ARE TOO VALUABLE TO BE WASTED ON ILL-CONCEIVED VENDETTAS. BESIDES, PAST ACTS WILL BE FORGOTTEN--
--ONCE YOU ARE IN THE EMPLOY OF *BOSS MUSORI.*
COME, LET ME SHOW YOU THE HOUSE YOU WILL SOON CALL HOME.
VERY NICE.
DO NOT BE FOOLED BY THE ELEGANCE. THIS IS THE HOME OF WARRIORS. OUR STRENGTH PAYS FOR THIS COMFORT.

YOUR DROID WILL HAVE TO WAIT OUTSIDE.

TYPICAL.

SILENCE, H2.

YOUR WEAPONS, DASS JENNIR. STRANGERS MAY NOT CARRY THEM ON THE PREMISES. YOU WILL HAVE NO NEED OF THEM.

OF COURSE.

I WILL INTRODUCE YOU TO BOSS MUSORI.

MASTER, I HAVE BROUGHT THE MAN -- THE STRANGER--

-- HE GOES BY THE NAME DASS JENNIR.

YOU BROUGHT HIM HERE?!

SILENCE. MORS DEMANNA HAS BROUGHT THIS MAN JENNIR AT MY REQUEST.

I HAVE HEARD OF YOUR PROWESS WITH A BLASTER. BUT, AS YOU NOW KNOW, WE JUDGE A WARRIOR BY HIS SKILL WITH A BLADE.

YOU SEEM FIT ENOUGH, FOR ONE OF YOUR SPECIES...

DEMANNA, TEST HIM!

77

FOR JENNIR, THE RING OF STEEL AGAINST STEEL IS A DISTRACTING NEW ELEMENT IN COMBAT.

A SWORD IS **NOT** A LIGHTSABER.

THE WEIGHT OF THE ATTACKER'S BLADE MAKES PARRYING IT MORE DIFFICULT --

-- EVEN AS THE HEFT OF HIS OWN BLADE SLOWS HIS COUNTERATTACK.

HE CAN STILL READ HIS OPPONENT'S INTENT THROUGH THE FORCE --

-- BUT EVASION AND DEFENSE ALONE WILL NOT IMPRESS HIS AUDIENCE.

FEAR NOT, JENNIR -- DEMANNA KNOWS NOT TO KILL YOU. HE WILL DO NO MORE THAN DRAW BLOOD.

TIME TO GO ON THE OFFENSIVE.

HEH.

PHFFF! IT IS BUT LUCK, NOT SKILL, HE DISPLAYS.

PERHAPS...

AND SO THE FIGHT GOES ON, NEITHER SIDE DRAWING BLOOD OR SCORING A "FATAL" POINT...

...UNTIL JENNIR DECIDES IT IS TIME TO BRING THE COMBAT TO A CLOSE.

HE SEES HIS OPENING, AND MAKES HIS FINAL ATTACK--

-- ONLY TO HAVE IT DENIED...

MASTER DEMANNA, I GIVE WAY. YOU HAVE BESTED ME.

FEEL NO SHAME IN DEFEAT, DASS JENNIR -- MORS DEMANNA HAS NEVER BEEN BEATEN.

HE IS VERY SKILLFUL. THERE ARE FEW LEFT IN THE GALAXY WHO ARE HIS EQUAL.

YES, HE IS A GREAT WARRIOR--AND AN *HONORABLE* ONE.

REALLY? HOW IS IT POSSIBLE THAT A SENTIENT CAN TRADE IN THE LIVES OF *HELPLESS* SLAVES AND STILL BELIEVE HE RETAINS *ANY* SEMBLANCE OF HONOR?

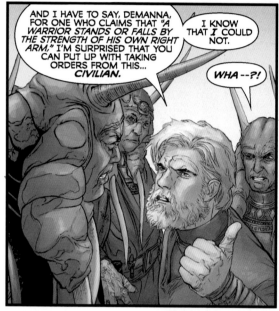

AND I HAVE TO SAY, DEMANNA, FOR ONE WHO CLAIMS THAT *"A WARRIOR STANDS OR FALLS BY THE STRENGTH OF HIS OWN RIGHT ARM,"* I'M SURPRISED THAT YOU CAN PUT UP WITH TAKING ORDERS FROM THIS... *CIVILIAN.*

I KNOW THAT *I* COULD NOT.

WHA--?!

NO MAN SAYS THAT TO ME AND LIVES!

DON'T MAKE THREATS YOU CAN'T FULFILL.

WE BOTH KNOW YOU WON'T STRIKE DOWN AN *UNARMED* MAN.

IT WOULDN'T BE...

...HONORABLE.

THAT DIDN'T TAKE LONG. I TRUST IT WENT WELL?

I KNOW, *"SHUT UP."*

THE MAN IS LEAVING THE SLAVERS' PLACE.

FOLLOW HIM. SEE WHERE HE GOES.

WE'RE BEING FOLLOWED.

NOT UNEXPECTED.

BY A T'SURRI.

HMM. INTERESTING. LET'S SEE HOW FAR HE'S WILLING TO GO.

THEY *MUST* HAVE HIRED HIM-- OTHERWISE HE'D BE BACK HERE BY NOW.

A MAN LIKE JENNIR WOULD NEVER ALIGN HIMSELF WITH SLAVERS...NOT AFTER WHAT THEY DID TO MY SON...

WHAT?! YOU ARE *NOT* TO INVOLVE JENNIR IN *YOUR* PROBLEMS! DO YOU *HEAR* ME?

BUT HE OFFERED TO HELP...

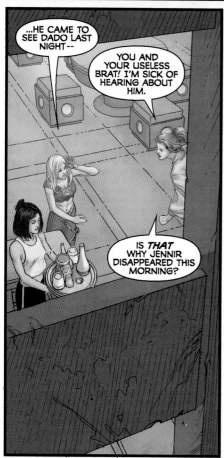

...HE CAME TO SEE DADO LAST NIGHT--

YOU AND YOUR USELESS BRAT! I'M SICK OF HEARING ABOUT HIM.

IS *THAT* WHY JENNIR DISAPPEARED THIS MORNING?

LISTEN, NIKOLLANE -- JENNIR IS AS MUCH MY SLAVE AS YOU ARE. YOU STAY AWAY FROM HIM!

SLAP!

HE HAS A JOB TO DO, AND UNTIL HE'S GOTTEN RID OF MUSORI AND HIS SLAVERS, YOU ARE NOT TO SPEAK TO HIM!

IF YOU *OR* YOUR SON INTERFERES WITH MY PLANS, I'LL SELL YOU TO THE HUTTS, AND TOSS THE KID INTO THE CANAL!

THE PLANET *KIDRON* -- ON THE OUTER-RIM LEG OF THE RIMMA TRADE ROUTE, NEAR THE *KURAS DRIFT.*

DOES IT *EVER* STOP RAINING HERE, RATTY?

WE USUALLY COME HERE DURING THE *DRY SEASON* -- TO LIE IN THE SUN AFTER A SUCCESSFUL JOB.

YEAH? WELL, IT HAS BEEN A WHILE SINCE WE'VE PULLED A JOB THAT ANYBODY COULD CALL *"SUCCESSFUL."*

AND WHEN YOU CAME HERE TO LIE IN THE SUN, DID CAPTAIN HEREN SPEND ALL OF HIS TIME--

-- DRUNK?

...LOOK, ISH LI'L BOMO GREEN -:*HIC*:- BARK...

DISGUSTING.

YOU HAVE TO UNDERSTAND, BOMO -- THE CAPTAIN BLAMES *HIMSELF* FOR ALL THAT HAS HAPPENED.

FUNNY, BECAUSE *I* BLAME HIM, TOO!

BOMO, THIS IS A DIFFICULT TIME FOR US ALL. GIVE THE CAPTAIN TIME -- WE'LL SOON GET BACK TO OUR REGULAR ROUTINE. HE'LL SNAP OUT OF IT. YOU'LL SEE.

HRM...

WELL, GOOD FOR HIM! TOO BAD *CRYS* AND *SNIFFLES* AND *JANKS* WILL NEVER BE ABLE TO "*SNAP OUT OF*" THE THINGS THAT HAPPENED TO THEM BECAUSE OF HEREN'S DECISIONS!

I WISH JENNIR WERE STILL WITH US...

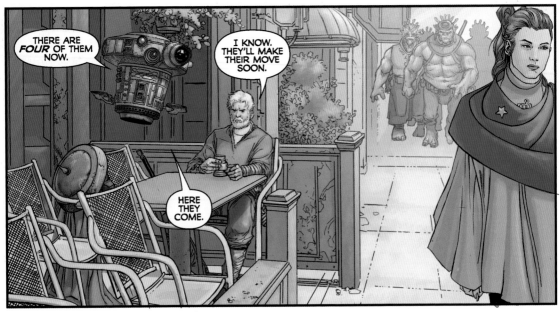

THERE ARE *FOUR* OF THEM NOW.

I KNOW. THEY'LL MAKE THEIR MOVE SOON.

HERE THEY COME.

AH, GENTLE BEINGS, HOW MAY I BE OF ASSISTANCE?

OUR BOSS WANTS TO TALK TO YOU. NOW.

BY ALL MEANS. I SHALL AWAIT THE PLEASURE OF HIS COMPANY.

NO! YOU WILL COME WITH US THIS MINUTE!

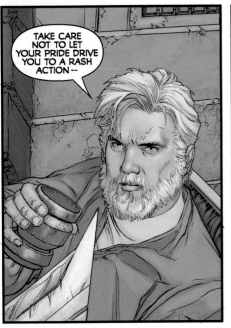

TAKE CARE NOT TO LET YOUR PRIDE DRIVE YOU TO A RASH ACTION --

-- YOU'LL *REGRET* IT.

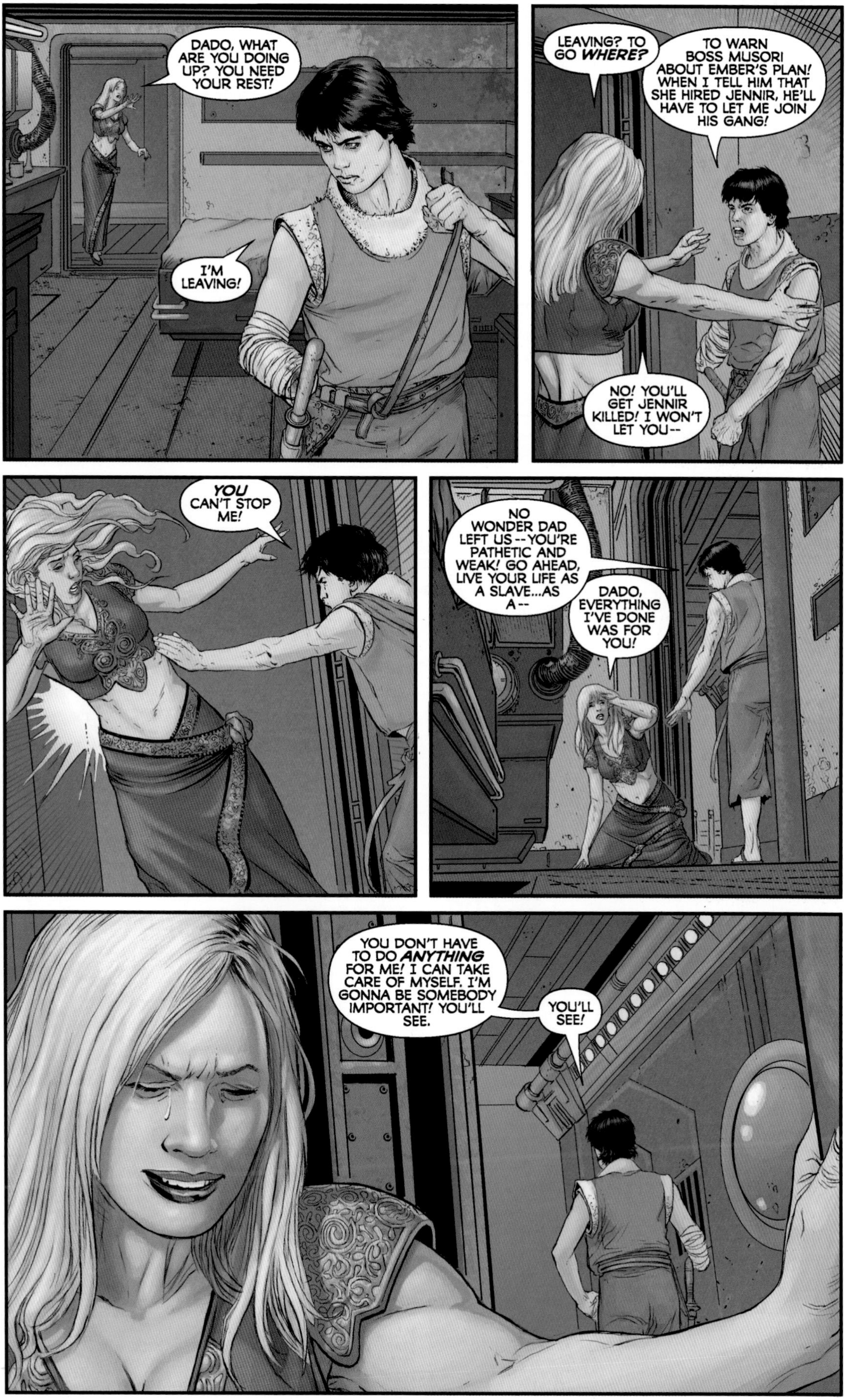
DADO, WHAT ARE YOU DOING UP? YOU NEED YOUR REST!
I'M LEAVING!
LEAVING? TO GO *WHERE?*
TO WARN BOSS MUSORI ABOUT EMBER'S PLAN! WHEN I TELL HIM THAT SHE HIRED JENNIR, HE'LL HAVE TO LET ME JOIN HIS GANG!
NO! YOU'LL GET JENNIR KILLED! I WON'T LET YOU--
YOU CAN'T STOP ME!
NO WONDER DAD LEFT US--YOU'RE PATHETIC AND WEAK! GO AHEAD, LIVE YOUR LIFE AS A SLAVE...AS A--
DADO, EVERYTHING I'VE DONE WAS FOR YOU!
YOU DON'T HAVE TO DO *ANYTHING* FOR ME! I CAN TAKE CARE OF MYSELF. I'M GONNA BE SOMEBODY IMPORTANT! YOU'LL SEE.
YOU'LL SEE!

YOU MUST BE *KEN-KIBA,* THE ONE THEY CALL *"BOSS."* I'M DASS JENNIR.

NEXT TIME YOU WISH TO SPEAK TO ME, I SUGGEST YOU COME IN PERSON--

--OR SEND MORE TROOPS.

HA-HA! THE STORIES WERE NOT EXAGGERATED-- IT SEEMS YOU ARE EVERYTHING THEY SAY!

IT'S NO WONDER MUSORI WANTS TO OFFER YOU A POSITION.

THE SLAVERS *DID* MAKE ME AN OFFER--

--BUT I TURNED THEM DOWN.

SIGNING ON AS AN ENFORCER IS ONE THING. BUT I DON'T WANT TO BE IN THE MIDDLE OF AN ALL-OUT WAR BETWEEN YOUR TWO GANGS.

WAR?

YOU HAVEN'T HEARD?

PERHAPS WE SHOULD CONTINUE THIS CONVERSATION INSIDE...

THIS WAY...

HMM. I CAN SEE WHY MUSORI IS SO CONFIDENT...

WHAT ARE YOU TALKING ABOUT?

I OVERHEARD MUSORI'S GUYS TALKING ABOUT TAKING OVER YOUR BUSINESS. AND FROM WHAT I'VE SEEN HERE, THEY COULD DO IT.

RIDICULOUS! MY SOLDIERS ARE MORE THAN A MATCH FOR THEIRS!

YOUR GUYS ARE TOUGHER, I'M SURE. BUT DISCIPLINE COUNTS FOR A LOT. SO DOES *SURPRISE.*

THE SLAVERS HAVE ALREADY MADE THE FIRST MOVE, AND YOU DON'T EVEN KNOW IT.

DEMANNA TOLD ME THEY TOOK OUT YOUR REFINERY LAST NIGHT.

WHAT?! *IMPOSSIBLE!*

SHIN-AY! GET ON THE COMM -- I WANT TO TALK TO MY BROTHER!

KEN-GIREE'S NOT RESPONDING, BOSS. NO ANSWER AT THE REFINERY AT ALL.

!

YOU! GRAB A FAST SHIP AND GET TO THE REFINERY. AND TAKE THOSE FOUR WORTHLESS IDIOTS IN THE COURTYARD WITH YOU!

YOU GOT IT, BOSS!

GET SOME HELP, ROUND UP THE TROOPS. HIT ALL THE CANTINAS AND THE USUAL HANGOUTS. TELL EVERYONE I WANT THEM HERE IN AN HOUR!

YES, BOSS!

WELL, GOOD LUCK, KEN-KIBA. I'LL BE ON MY WAY.

LIKE I SAID, I DON'T WANT TO GET CAUGHT IN THE MIDDLE OF A WAR.

COME ON, H2. THINGS WILL BEGIN TO HAPPEN VERY QUICKLY NOW.

I THINK I'M BEGINNING TO LIKE YOU, MAN-WHO-KILLED-MY-MASTER.

KIDRON.

THE WAR IS OVER, BUT ALL OF THE GREATEST TRAGEDIES OF BOMO GREENBARK'S LIFE HAVE HAPPENED IN THE FOUR SHORT MONTHS SINCE THE REPUBLIC -- NOW THE EMPIRE -- DECLARED VICTORY AND PEACE.

NOT A DAY -- SCARCELY AN HOUR -- GOES BY THAT HE DOESN'T DWELL ON THAT LIST, THE THOUGHT OF ONE LOSS REMINDING HIM OF ALL OF THE OTHERS. IT IS A LITANY THAT DOES NOT BECOME EASIER BY REPETITION...

...EACH RECITAL REFRESHING THE WOUNDS...

...COMPOUNDING THE PAIN.

HIS FELLOW NOSAURIANS WERE SLAUGHTERED BY THE CLONE TROOPERS...

...HIS BELOVED WIFE, MESA, KILLED BY SLAVERS ON ORVAX IV...

...RESA...DARLING RESA... THEIR ONLY CHILD, TAKEN BY THE MAN CALLED DEZONO QUA AND --

I HOPE YOU'RE HUNGRY, BOMO! I DECIDED TO COOK UP ALL OF THE GORKA THIGHS BEFORE THEY WENT BAD!

UGH...

I CAN'T EAT RIGHT NOW, RATTY...

...I'M GOING FOR A WALK.

AND THE TRAGIC REVIEW CONTINUES...

...THE CREW OF THE UHUMELE -- HIS NEWFOUND REPLACEMENT FAMILY -- FALLING ONE BY ONE...

...JANKS TAKEN BY THE EMPIRE... SNIFFLES SHOT BY SMUGGLERS... CRYS HORRIBLY TRANSFORMED --

HUH?

BOMO GREENBARK?

I HAVE BEEN LOOKING FOR YOU. MY NAME IS *BEYGHOR SAHDETT,* AND I BELIEVE WE SHARE A MUTUAL ACQUAINTANCE...

DASS JENNIR!

WHERE HAVE YOU BEEN? WHAT HAVE YOU BEEN DO--

I--*UH,* I WAS SO WORRIED ABOUT YOU.

HAVE YOU MADE ANY PROGRESS WITH BOSS MUSORI?

SOME...

...BUT I'VE MADE EVEN *MORE* WITH *KEN-KIBA* AND HIS SPICE RUNNERS.

YOUR GANG PROBLEMS SHOULD BE OVER SOON.

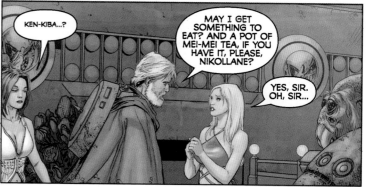

KEN-KIBA...?

MAY I GET SOMETHING TO EAT? AND A POT OF MEI-MEI TEA, IF YOU HAVE IT, PLEASE, NIKOLLANE?

YES, SIR. OH, SIR...

...I'M SO WORRIED. MY BOY DADO HAS RUN OFF TO TRY TO JOIN THE SLAVERS -- BOSS MUSORI'S GANG -- AGAIN.

I DIDN'T BELIEVE WHAT MISTRESS EMBER SAID, BUT DADO OVERHEARD IT, AND --

WHAT DID SHE SAY?

THAT YOU WERE HERE TO RID US OF THE SLAVERS -- THAT SHE HIRED YOU TO INFILTRATE THE GANG --

STAY HERE, H2.

NIKOLLANE, *WHAT* DID YOU SAY TO HIM?

ANSWER ME!

GET TO THE POINT! WHAT HAVE YOU FOUND AT THE REFINERY?

IT'S NOT GOOD, SHIN-AY --KEN-KIBA ISN'T GONNA BE HAPPY. WE FOUND HIS BROTHER...

...THE REFINERY'S BEEN TORCHED... KEN-GIREE'S DEAD --ALL OF OUR GUYS ARE!

WHAT?!

THEY WAS SHOT, BOSS -- EVERY ONE OF THEM. GUNNED DOWN WITHOUT A CHANCE!

AND WE GOT PROOF IT WAS THE SLAVERS THAT DID IT! BOSS --

"-- I THINK MUSORI'S 'HONOR' AND 'SWORD LAW' STUFF WAS ALL PART OF A SETUP!"

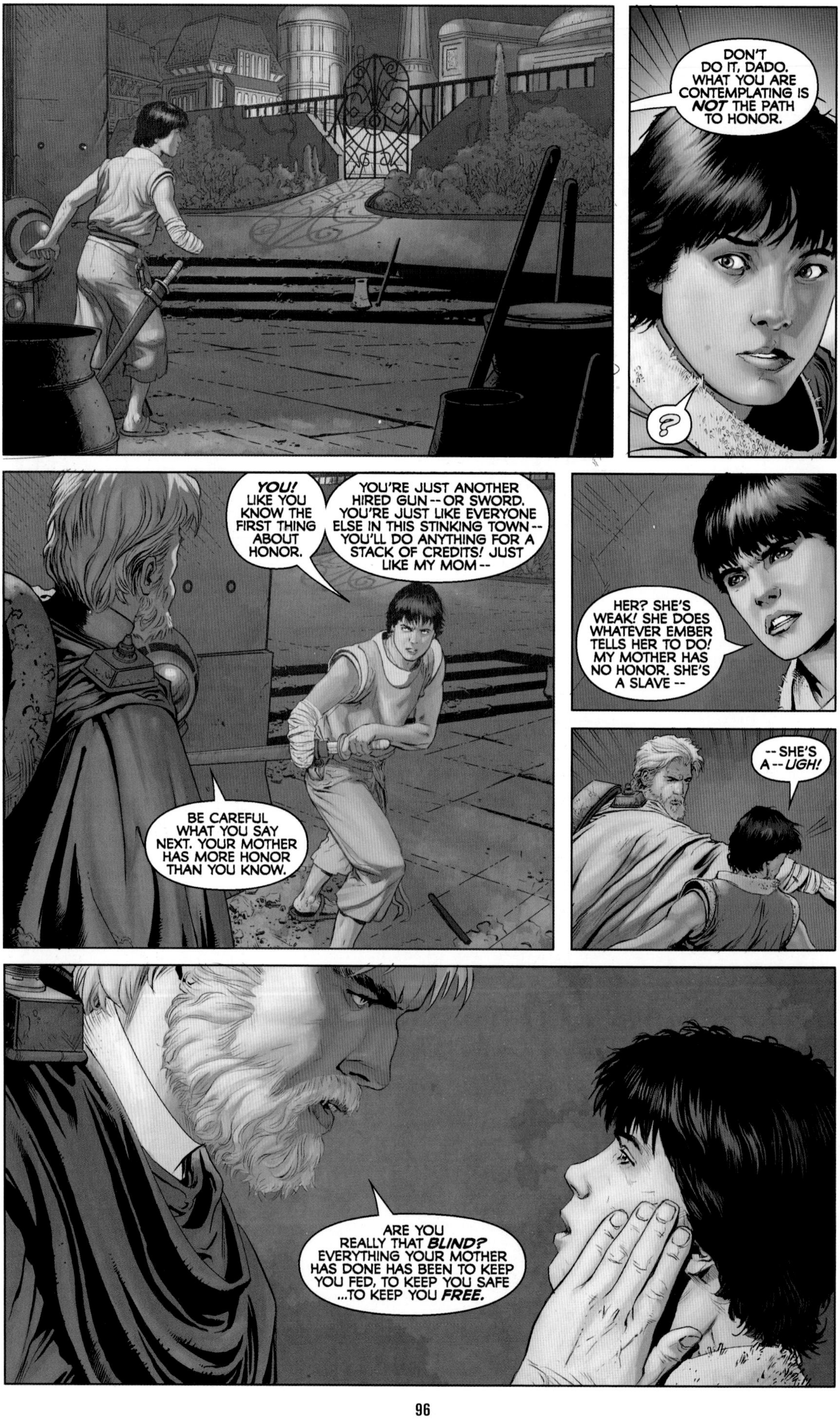
DON'T DO IT, DADO. WHAT YOU ARE CONTEMPLATING IS NOT THE PATH TO HONOR.
?
YOU! LIKE YOU KNOW THE FIRST THING ABOUT HONOR.
YOU'RE JUST ANOTHER HIRED GUN--OR SWORD. YOU'RE JUST LIKE EVERYONE ELSE IN THIS STINKING TOWN--YOU'LL DO ANYTHING FOR A STACK OF CREDITS! JUST LIKE MY MOM--
BE CAREFUL WHAT YOU SAY NEXT. YOUR MOTHER HAS MORE HONOR THAN YOU KNOW.
HER? SHE'S WEAK! SHE DOES WHATEVER EMBER TELLS HER TO DO! MY MOTHER HAS NO HONOR. SHE'S A SLAVE--
--SHE'S A--UGH!
ARE YOU REALLY THAT BLIND? EVERYTHING YOUR MOTHER HAS DONE HAS BEEN TO KEEP YOU FED, TO KEEP YOU SAFE ...TO KEEP YOU FREE.

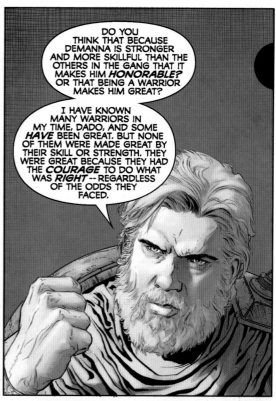

DO YOU THINK THAT BECAUSE DEMANNA IS STRONGER AND MORE SKILLFUL THAN THE OTHERS IN THE GANG THAT IT MAKES HIM *HONORABLE?* OR THAT BEING A WARRIOR MAKES HIM GREAT?

I HAVE KNOWN MANY WARRIORS IN MY TIME, DADO, AND SOME *HAVE* BEEN GREAT. BUT NONE OF THEM WERE MADE GREAT BY THEIR SKILL OR STRENGTH. THEY WERE GREAT BECAUSE THEY HAD THE *COURAGE* TO DO WHAT WAS *RIGHT* -- REGARDLESS OF THE ODDS THEY FACED.

ALL OF HER SACRIFICES -- EVEN TO THE POINT OF GIVING UP HER OWN FREEDOM -- HAVE BEEN MADE BECAUSE SHE LOVES *YOU* MORE THAN HERSELF.

WITHOUT SACRIFICE, THERE CAN BE NO HONOR.

YOU IDOLIZE DEMANNA, BUT DO YOU THINK *HE* WOULD MAKE SUCH A SACRIFICE? DEMANNA IS ALL ABOUT DEMANNA. HE IS CONSUMED WITH PRIDE -- AND *THAT* WILL EVENTUALLY BE HIS DOWNFALL.

KNOW THIS -- PRIDE IS MOTIVATED BY *FEAR* -- FEAR OF WHAT OTHERS THINK OF YOU. WHEN YOU ALLOW ANOTHER'S *OPINION* OF YOU TO CONTROL YOUR ACTIONS RATHER THAN DOING WHAT YOU KNOW TO BE RIGHT, THEN YOU ARE TRULY A SLAVE.

SOMEDAY YOU'LL UNDERSTAND, I'M SURE. BUT RIGHT NOW --

"-- WE'RE ABOUT TO SEE A FIGHT BETWEEN WARRIORS WHO ARE DRIVEN BY PRIDE AND FEAR AND GREED."

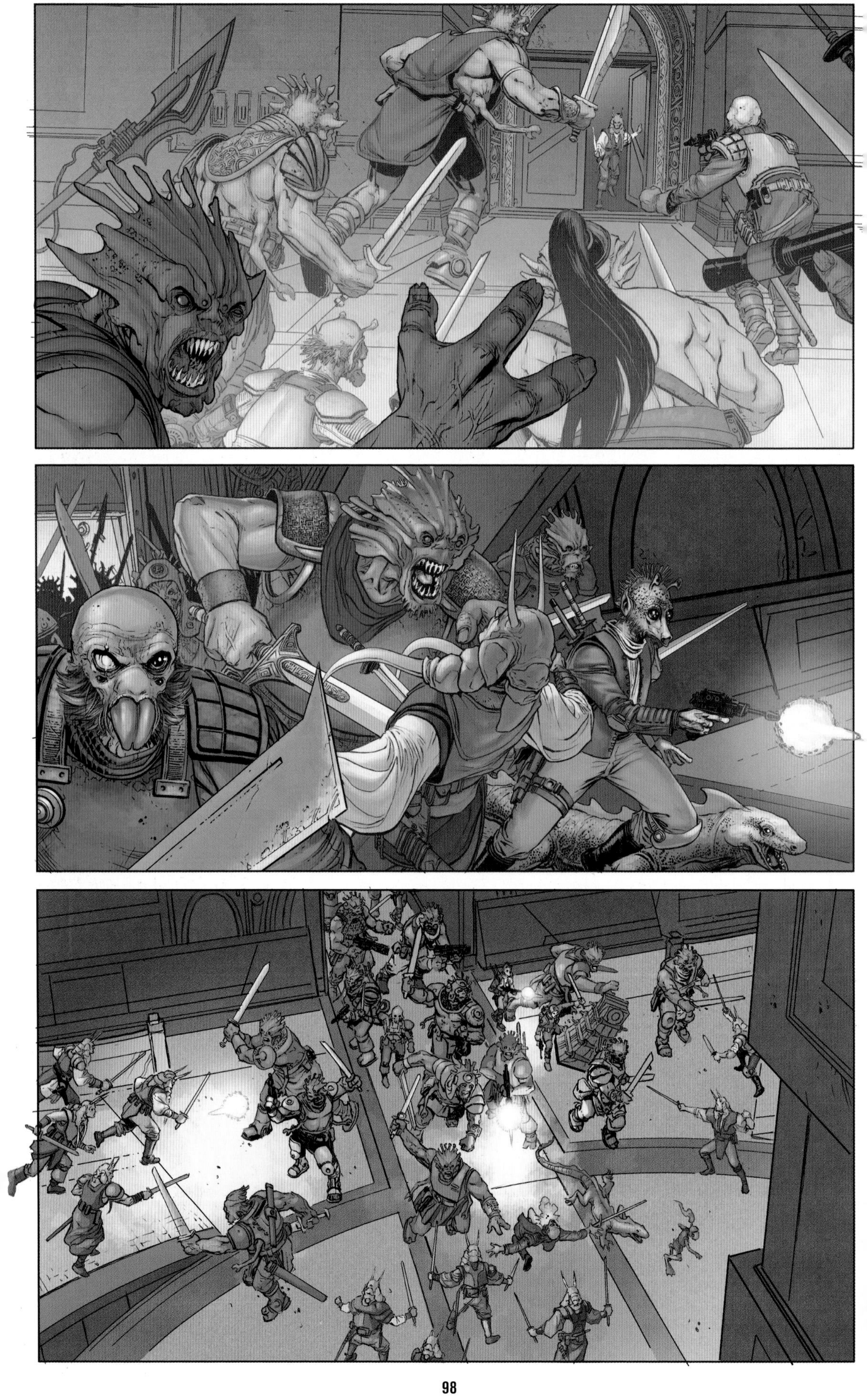

SPANG!

KANG!

THEY'RE USING BLASTERS -- AND *GRENADES!*

THEY'VE BROKEN THE *SWORD LAW!*

THIS FIGHT HAS NOTHING TO DO WITH HONOR OR LEGITIMATE DISPUTES. THIS IS ABOUT ONE SIDE WANTING TO *DESTROY* THE OTHER.

THIS IS WHAT *WAR* IS ALL ABOUT.

THERE'S NOTHING GLORIOUS ABOUT IT.

KEN-KIBA -- WHY ARE YOU DOING THIS?! WE HAD AN AGREEMENT -- A *TREATY!*

WE HAVE SWORD LAW!

DOW!
BDOW!
SHRAK!
DOW!

THIS IS AN OUTRAGE! DEMANNA -- RALLY THE MEN, LEAD A COUNTERATTACK!

A *COUNTERATTACK?*

HURRY! IT'S OUR ONLY CHANCE!

YOU MEAN *YOUR* ONLY CHANCE.

YOU WOULD SEND ALL THOSE MEN TO THEIR DEATHS? WHAT OF HONOR?

WHAT OF IT? THEY ARE PAID TO DO AS THEY'RE TOLD -- THEY ARE *MINE* TO COMMAND.

TELL THEM I'LL DOUBLE THEIR SALARIES -- NO, *TRIPLE* THEM.

DEAD MEN CAN DRAW NO SALARIES.

JUST DO IT!

GIVE ME THREE MINUTES TO WORK MY WAY DOWNSTAIRS, THEN CONCENTRATE YOUR ATTACK ON THE FRONT OF THE HOUSE.

THREE MINUTES HAVE PASSED. WHERE ARE THE SOUNDS OF THE ATTACK HE ORDERED?

COULD SOMETHING HAVE GONE --

-- WRONG?

WE GOT MUSORI!

WHAT ABOUT DEMANNA?

"NO SIGN OF HIM, BOSS."

DOESN'T MATTER. MUSORI'S THE *REAL* PRIZE --

KEN-KIBA!

WHAT IS IT, WOMAN?

I HAVE INFORMATION-- SOMETHING YOU SHOULD KNOW!

NIKOLLANE! EVERYBODY! YOU'VE GOT TO GET OUT -- NOW!

DADO!

LISTEN TO ME -- YOU MUST LEAVE! GET OUT OF HERE. WAR HAS BROKEN OUT BETWEEN THE SPICERS AND THE SLAVERS. THIS INN WILL NO LONGER BE NEUTRAL GROUND!

BUT WHERE WILL WE GO?

AWAY FROM THE CITY.

DADO, GO WITH YOUR MOTHER. KEEP HER SAFE.

YOU WANT TO EARN HONOR? NOW IS THE TIME FOR YOU TO STEP UP -- PROTECT YOUR MOTHER AS SHE HAS PROTECTED YOU ALL THESE YEARS.

HURRY NOW! GET AWAY--

I DON'T THINK SO.

THE WOMEN ARE STAYING. I PAID FOR THEM. THEY'RE MY PROPERTY.

AND YOU, JENNIR, ARE ALL MINE.

GRAB HIM! I'LL MOUNT HIS HEAD NEXT TO MUSORI'S!

MY MASTER -- THE CHAMPION OF LOST CAUSES.

YOU'RE THE ONE WHO *STARTED* ALL OF THIS.

KLOK!

STIRRED EVERYBODY UP--

--KILLED MY BROTHER--

WHUD!

--DESTROYED OUR REFINERY--

KRAK!

--AND CAUSED ME TO EXPEND VALUABLE RESOURCES FIGHTING A WAR WITH THE SLAVERS!

GET HIM ON HIS FEET!

THE THING IS, I GOT WHAT I WANTED. I NOW CONTROL THE WHOLE TOWN -- INCLUDING ALL OF THE SLAVERS' OPERATIONS.

BUT IT COST ME TOO MUCH!

SO, BEFORE I TAKE YOUR HEAD, I'M GOING TO TAKE AS MUCH OUT OF YOUR HIDE AS I CAN.

GOOD LUCK WITH THAT.

LUCK?! I DON'T NEED LUCK--

--I HAVE YOU!

NOT FOR LONG...

KLICK

?!

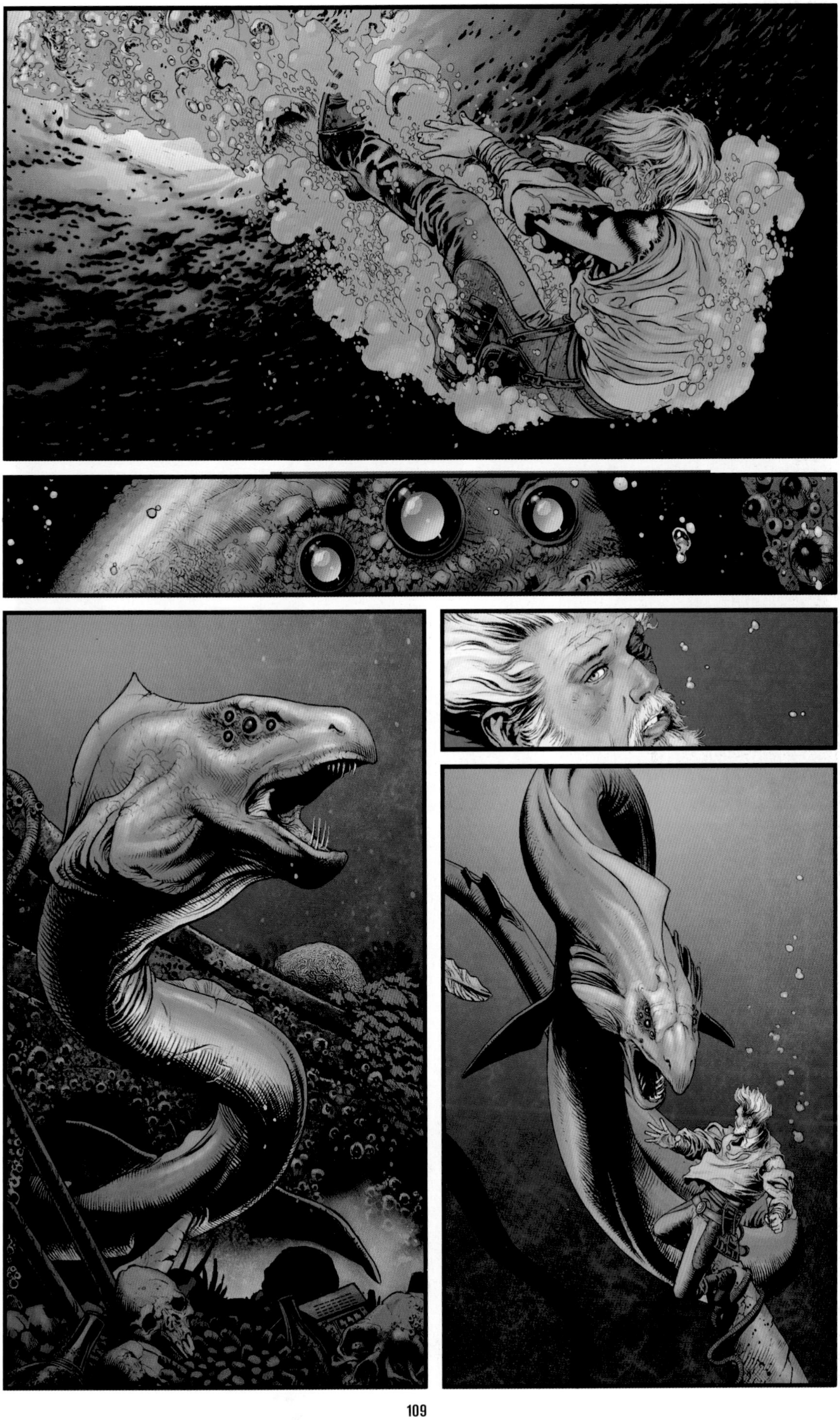

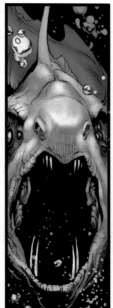

≥GASP!≤

I GOTCHA, CAP'N!

YOU LEAVE EVERYTHING TO OL' FISH.

GOOD THING YOU SENT YOUR DROID. HE GOT TO ME JUST IN *TIME!*

HE HAD A BOAT, BOSS! HE GOT AWAY!

?!

WE'LL CATCH HIM EVENTUALLY. IN THE MEANTIME, WE STILL HAVE HIS ACCOMPLICES --

--INCLUDING *YOU,* EMBER CHANKEL!

ME?

I WAS *HELPING* YOU! *I* WAS THE ONE WHO TOLD YOU WHAT JENNIR WAS DOING--

AFTER IT WAS TOO LATE! NOW THAT I THINK ABOUT IT, *YOU'RE* THE ONE WHO BROUGHT JENNIR HERE IN THE FIRST PLACE. *YOU'RE* THE ONE WHO ASSURED ME THAT HE WAS *"EASILY MANIPULATED."*

NOW I HAVE TO WONDER *WHO* YOU THOUGHT YOU WERE *MANIPULATING!*

LOCK HER UP WITH THE OTHERS. I'LL FIGURE OUT WHAT TO DO WITH THEM LATER.

THE REST OF YOU--*FIND* JENNIR!

THE NEXT MORNING...

HHUUUH...

SO, YOU *ARE* ALIVE.

EASY, CAP'N. YOU'RE IN NO SHAPE TO BE SITTIN' UP.

WHERE--?

MY PLACE -- OUT AT THE END OF THE ARCHIPELAGO. WE'VE BEEN LAYIN' LOW SINCE I PULLED YOU OUTTA THE CANAL.

WHAT ABOUT NIKOLLANE, AND HER SON? WHAT ABOUT... EMBER?

THE NEWS FROM TOWN ISN'T GOOD...

...ESPECIALLY FOR THE SLAVERS.

KEN-KIBA AND HIS BOYS HAVE ROUNDED UP ALL OF MUSORI'S GANG AND PUT THEIR HEADS ON PIKES. ALL OF 'EM BUT DEMANNA, THAT IS. THEY HAVEN'T FOUND HIM.

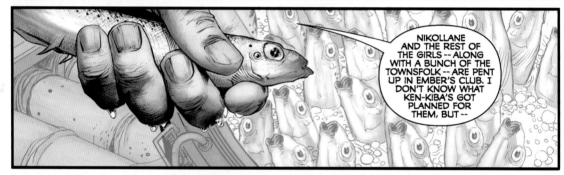

NIKOLLANE AND THE REST OF THE GIRLS -- ALONG WITH A BUNCH OF THE TOWNSFOLK -- ARE PENT UP IN EMBER'S CLUB. I DON'T KNOW WHAT KEN-KIBA'S GOT PLANNED FOR THEM, BUT --

-- MY GUESS IS IT'S THE SAME KIND OF TORTURE EMBER CHANKELI GOT --

-- AND THE SAME THAT HE HAS IN MIND FOR YOU AND ME -- IF HE FINDS US.

EVERY SPICER HE CAN SPARE IS OUT SEARCHIN'.

IF YOU'VE BEEN HIDING OUT HERE, HOW DO YOU KNOW SO MUCH ABOUT WHAT'S BEEN HAPPENING IN TOWN?

YOUR DROID. HE WAS FERRYIN' REPORTS BACK ALL NIGHT--

--UNTIL HE GOT SHOT. HE MANAGED TO HAUL YOUR SWORD HERE ...BEFORE HE SHUT DOWN FOR GOOD.

NOT THAT THAT SWORD WILL DO YOU MUCH GOOD. 'KIBA'S BOYS PUT A HURT ON YOU.

I FELT YOUR RIBS -- IT'LL BE A WEEK BEFORE YOU'RE EVEN ON YOUR FEET.

DON'T COUNT ME OUT YET, OLD MAN. I JUST NEED SOME SLEEP...

JENNIR HAS HAD SOME EXPERIENCE WITH "HEALING TRANCES." HE KNOWS WHAT THEY CAN DO...

...AND WHAT THEY CAN'T. BUT IT IS THE ONLY OPTION LEFT TO HIM IF HE IS TO AVOID FAILING THE PEOPLE OF NOLA --

...I KNOW WHAT I SAID, BUT I WAS DISTRAUGHT. I HAD LOST MY WIFE AND MY DAUGHTER!

MEZGRAF, YOU'RE WITH ME, RIGHT?

I DON'T KNOW, BOMO...

I'M FOR IT! HAVING A **JEDI** ON BOARD COULD BE--

TROUBLE IS WHAT IT COULD BE, RATTY.

YOU **ALWAYS** SIDE WITH BOMO -- NO MATTER WHAT.

PHFF!

KO VAKIER'S RIGHT. WHADDA WE **KNOW** ABOUT HIM?

HOW DO WE KNOW ‡URP!‡--

--WHATSISNAME'S EVEN A JEDI?

THE NAME IS **BEYGHOR SAHDETT,** AND I ASSURE YOU, CAPTAIN HEREN, I **AM** A JEDI.

I'M RECEIVING CONFIRMATION, SIR. THIS *IS* THE GROUP THAT HARBORED GENERAL JENNIR.

ALL RIGHT. *MOVE IN!*

HANDS UP! IN THE NAME OF THE EMPEROR!

TROOPERS!

SAHDETT--?

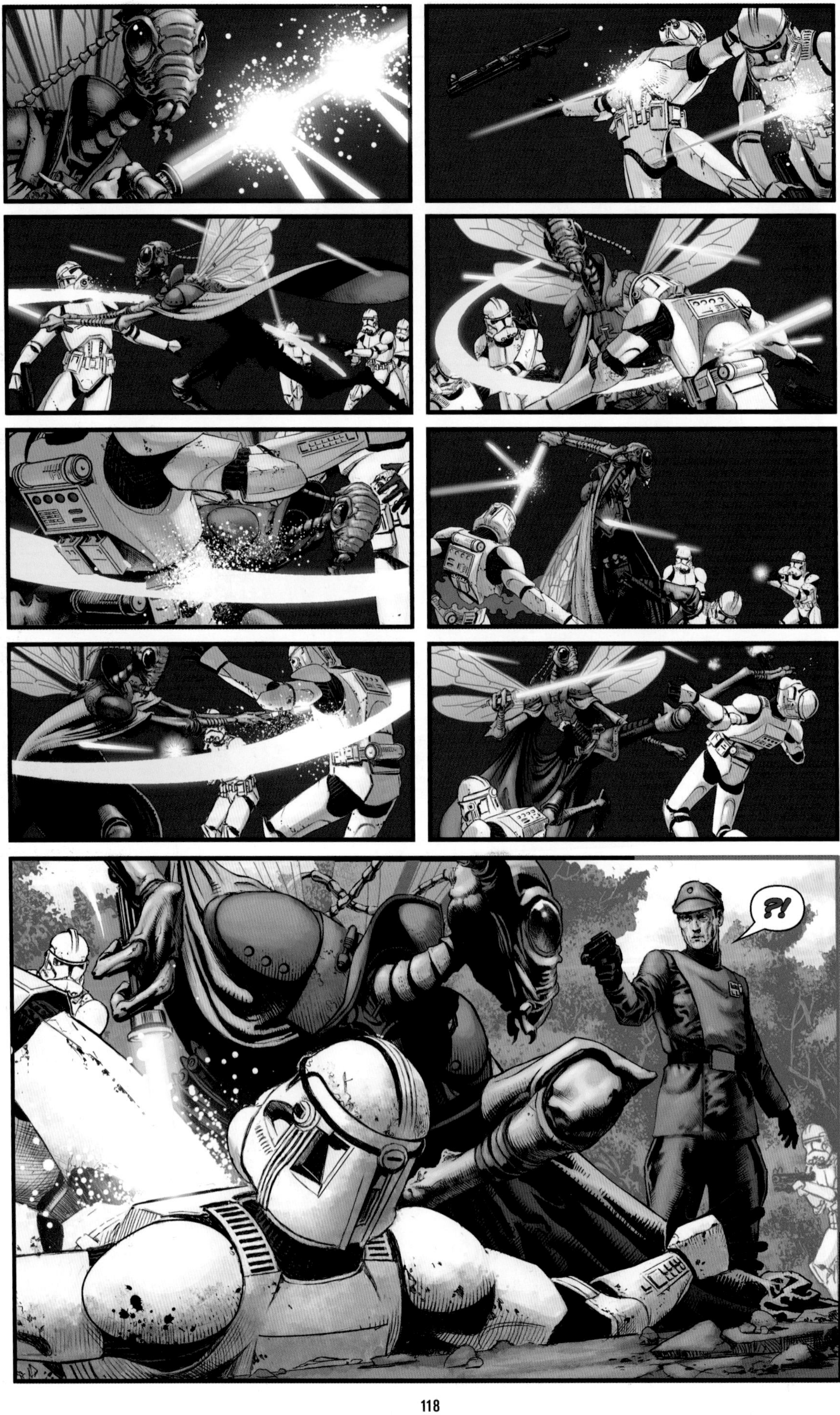
?!

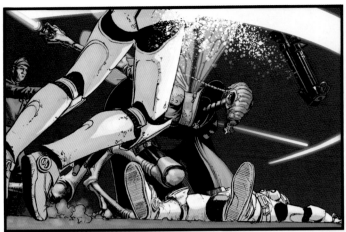

ZDOW!

BUT...

SKOW!

...!

ALL RIGHT, SO HE *IS* A JEDI...

HOPE YOU LIKE EEL--

--!

WHAT D'YA THINK YOU'RE DOING? YOU SHOULDN'T BE UP--

I FEEL LIKE A *NEW* MAN, FISH. I THOUGHT I SHOULD *LOOK* THE PART.

BUT YOUR RIBS WERE *BROKEN*...

STILL ARE. BUT THEY'RE HEALING.

NO, I MEANT...I FEEL *RENEWED*-- MENTALLY, IF NOT PHYSICALLY.

FOR THE FIRST TIME IN A LONG TIME, WHAT I *HAVE* TO DO AND WHAT I *SHOULD* DO ARE THE SAME.

AND JUST WHAT IS IT THAT YOU THINK YOU *HAVE* TO DO?

STOP KEN-KIBA. SAVE THE TOWNSPEOPLE.

I CAN'T LET OTHERS SUFFER BECAUSE OF SOMETHING I STARTED.

AW, HELL --YOU DIDN'T *START* NOTHING! BEFORE 'KIBA IT WAS --

UH-OH. SKIMMERS COMIN'!

RRRRRRRRRR

I'LL TRY TO DISTRACT THEM, CAP'N!

FISH, NO --!

THIS IS PRIVATE PROPERTY --!

SHUT UP!

CHECK THE SHACK!

RIGHT.

HUH.

LOOKS LIKE WE INTERRUPTED DINNER. ≩MUNCH!≩

NOTHIN' IN THERE BUT THAT SHOT-UP DROID. NO SIGN OF JENNIR-- BUT THE OLD MAN WILL TELL US WHERE HE IS.

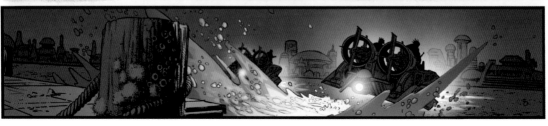

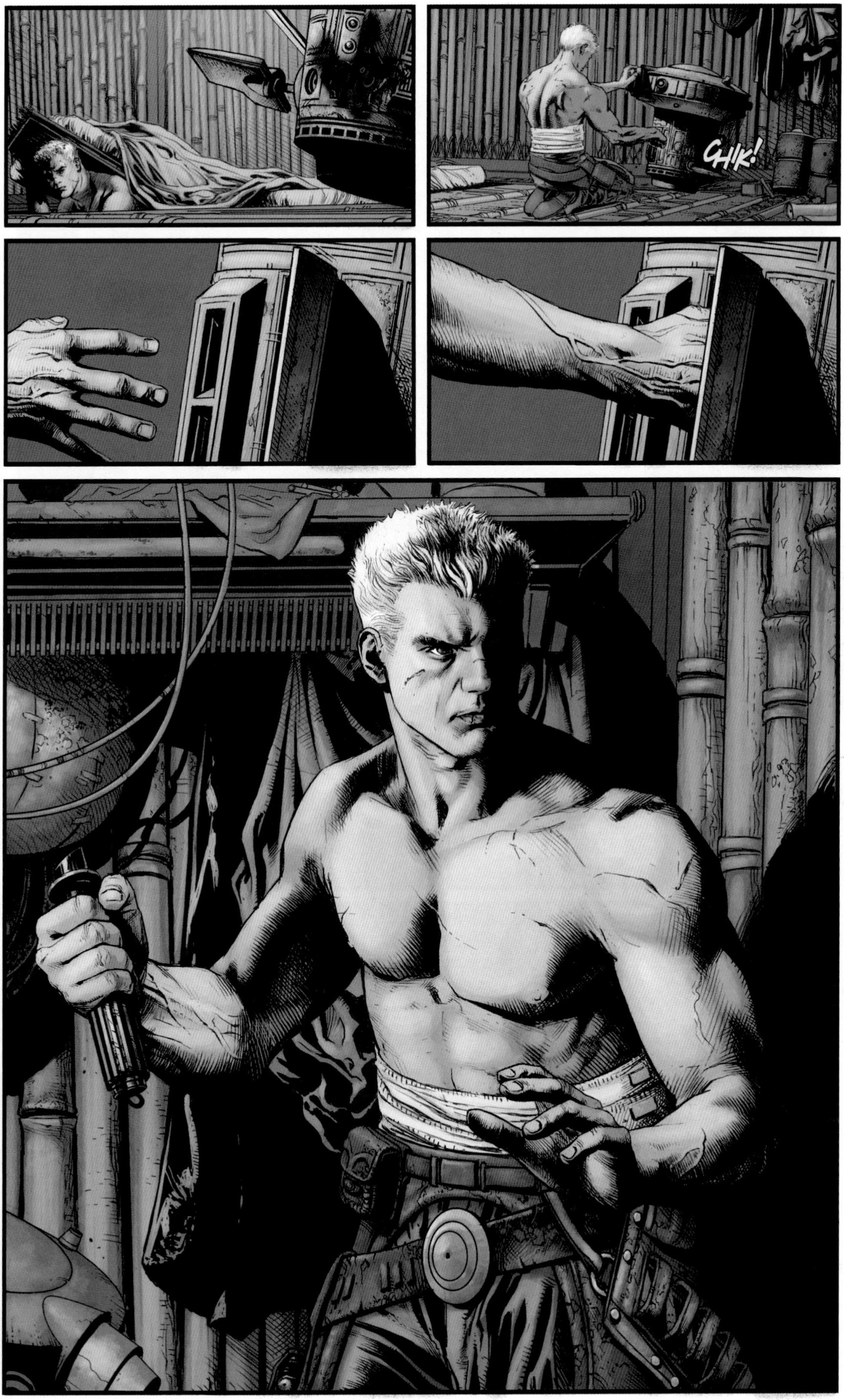
CHIK!

THUNK!

?

WHAT'S GOIN' ON OUT THERE?

I THINK I CAN GRAB HIS BLASTER...

DADO, NO!

HUK!

WHA--?!

BDOW!

DASS JENNIR!

TIME TO GO, FOLKS.

TAKE WHATEVER BOATS OR SKIMMERS YOU CAN FIND. HEAD FOR THE OUTER ISLANDS.

JUST GET OUT OF TOWN.

BUT-- WHAT ABOUT YOU?

I STILL HAVE SOME BUSINESS TO TAKE CARE OF.

IT'S YOU.

I'M GLAD YOU LIVED TO SEE THE DAMAGE YOU CAUSED.

I PLAN TO LIVE TO SEE THE DAMAGE *YOU* CAUSED REPAIRED. I--

...

WHAT IS IT?

DEMANNA.

JENNIR. I WAS AFRAID YOU HAD RUN AWAY.

I WAS TOLD *YOU* HAD.

I WILL SOON DEPART. BUT NOT BEFORE WE SETTLE THINGS BETWEEN US.

YOU HAVE *DESTROYED* MY LIFE -- ROBBED ME OF MY *POSITION* AND MY *HONOR.* I WILL HAVE SATISFACTION.

YOU'VE CONFUSED *POSITION* FOR RESPECT, AND *PRIDE* FOR HONOR. HONOR IS THE ONE THING NO ONE CAN *TAKE* FROM YOU--

--AS LONG AS YOU CONDUCT YOURSELF *HONORABLY.*

I DON'T WISH TO FIGHT YOU, DEMANNA. DON'T THROW AWAY YOUR LIFE AS WELL AS YOUR HONOR.

SILENCE! I BESTED YOU BEFORE. THIS TIME I WILL SHOW NO MERCY!

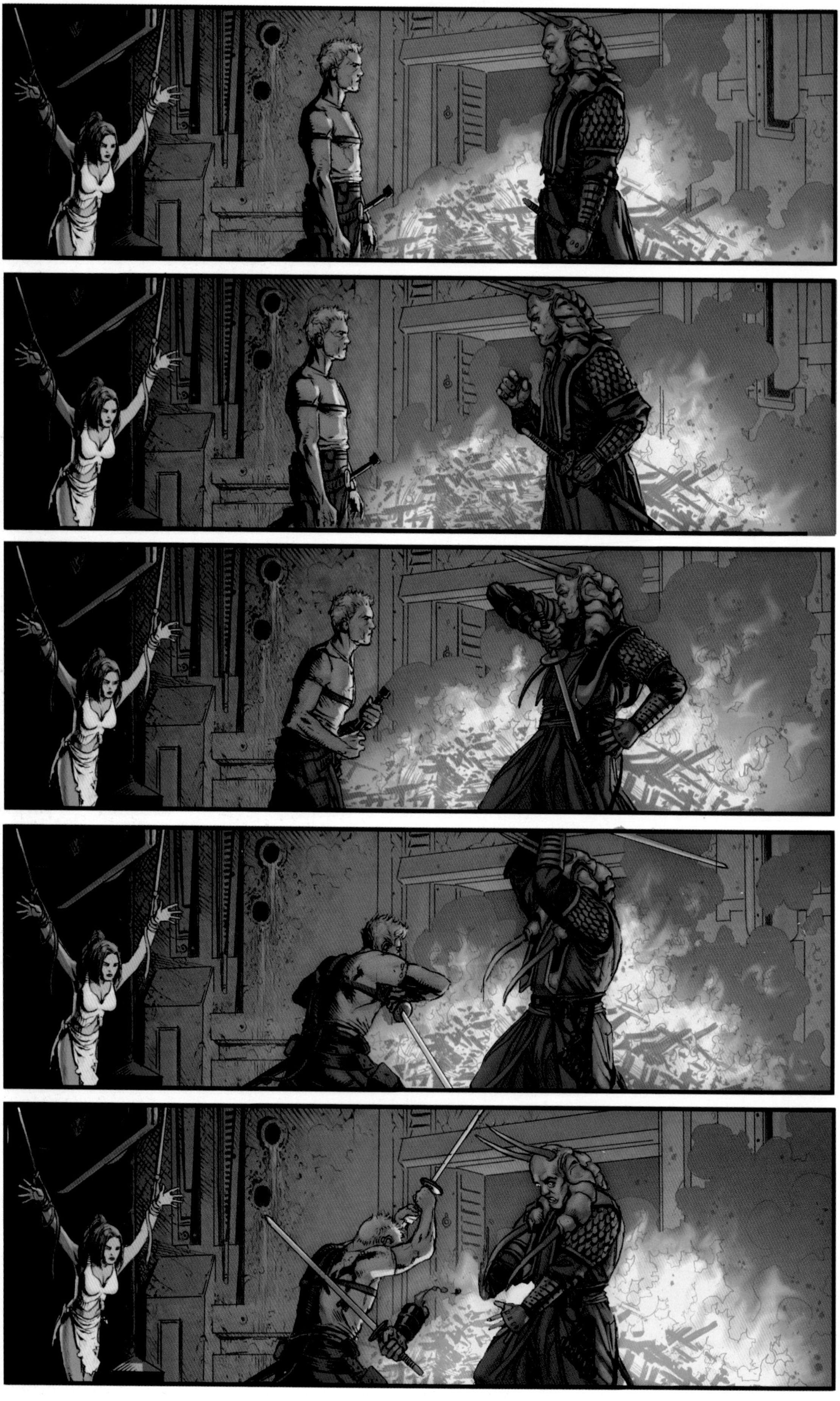

MY HAND--!

BUT WHEN WE FOUGHT BEFORE... YOU...

I ALLOWED YOU TO WIN. I PLAYED ON YOUR PRIDE.

CURSE YOU.

YOU HAVE WON. I *DEMAND* THAT YOU *FINISH* THIS. KILL ME.

I REFUSE.

SO CRUEL. YOU WOULD LEAVE ME WITH NOTHING?

I'M LEAVING YOU WITH YOUR LIFE -- AND A CHANCE TO REGAIN YOUR HONOR.

BUT TRY TO DO IT WITHOUT THE PRIDE.

129

SO, ANOTHER FOE VANQUISHED. YOUR VICTORY IS COMPLETE.

NOT QUITE.

!

MORE *MERCY?* YOU'RE FULL OF SURPRISES.

WHERE ARE YOU GOING?

DON'T GO DOWN THERE!

THE SPICERS--!

JENNIR!

YOU'RE GOING TO GET YOURSELF KILLED!

JENNIR...

SOONER OR LATER, OLD MAN, YOU'LL TELL US WHERE TO FIND JENNIR.

DO YOUR WORST...

OH, WE *WILL.*

GIVE 'IM ANOTHER LASH!

HURK!

?!

I GUESS
YOU KNOW
NOW WHERE
TO FIND
HIM...

THEY'RE GOING TO *KILL* YOU!

WHY ARE YOU DOING THIS?

VVVVIIIIIII

IT'S MY JOB.

THE END

STAR WARS GRAPHIC NOVEL TIMELINE (IN YEARS)

Omnibus: Tales of the Jedi—5,000–3,986 BSW4

Knights of the Old Republic (9 volumes)—3,964 BSW4

Jedi vs. Sith—1,000 BSW4

Omnibus: Rise of the Sith—33 BSW4

Episode I: The Phantom Menace—32 BSW4

Omnibus: Emissaries and Assassins—32 BSW4

Bounty Hunters—31 BSW4

Omnibus: Quinlan Vos – Jedi in Darkness—31–28 BSW4

Omnibus: Menace Revealed—31–22 BSW4

Honor and Duty—24 BSW4

Episode II: Attack of the Clones—22 BSW4

Clone Wars (9 volumes)—22–19 BSW4

Clone Wars Adventures (10 volumes)—22–19 BSW4

The Clone Wars (7 volumes)—22–19 BSW4

General Grievous—20 BSW4

Episode III: Revenge of the Sith—19 BSW4

Dark Times (4 volumes)—19 BSW4

Omnibus: Droids—3 BSW4

Omnibus: Boba Fett—3–1 BSW4, 0–10 ASW4

The Force Unleashed—2 BSW4

Adventures (4 volumes)—1–0 BSW4, 0–3 ASW4

Episode IV: A New Hope—SW4

Classic Star Wars—0–3 ASW4

A Long Time Ago… (7 volumes)—0–4 ASW4

Empire (6 volumes)—0 ASW4

Rebellion (3 volumes)—0 ASW4

Omnibus: Early Victories—0–1 ASW4

Jabba the Hutt: The Art of the Deal—1 ASW4

Episode V: The Empire Strikes Back—3 ASW4

Omnibus: Shadows of the Empire—3.5–4.5 ASW4

Episode VI: Return of the Jedi—4 ASW4

Omnibus: X-Wing Rogue Squadron—4–5 ASW4

The Thrawn Trilogy—9 ASW4

Dark Empire—10 ASW4

Crimson Empire—11 ASW4

Jedi Academy: Leviathan—13 ASW4

Union—20 ASW4

Chewbacca—25 ASW4

Legacy (10 volumes)—130 ASW4

Old Republic Era
25,000 – 1000 years before
Star Wars: A New Hope

Rise of the Empire Era
1000 – 0 years before
Star Wars: A New Hope

Rebellion Era
0 – 5 years after
Star Wars: A New Hope

New Republic Era
5 – 25 years after
Star Wars: A New Hope

New Jedi Order Era
25+ years after
Star Wars: A New Hope

Legacy Era
130+ years after
Star Wars: A New Hope

Infinities
Does not apply to timeline

Sergio Aragonés Stomps Star Wars
Star Wars Tales
Star Wars Infinities
Tag and Bink
Star Wars Visionaries

BSW4 = before *Episode IV: A New Hope*. ASW4 = after *Episode IV: A New Hope*.

STAR WARS VECTOR

An event with repercussions for every era and every hero in the *Star Wars* galaxy begins here! For anyone who never knew where to start with *Star Wars* comics, *Vector* is the perfect introduction to the entire *Star Wars* line! For any serious *Star Wars* fan, *Vector* is a must-see event with major happenings throughout the most important moments of the galaxy's history!

VOLUME ONE
(*Knights of the Old Republic* Vol. 5; *Dark Times* Vol. 3)
ISBN 978-1-59582-226-0 | $17.99

VOLUME TWO
(*Rebellion* Vol. 4; *Legacy* Vol. 6)
ISBN 978-1-59582-227-7 | $17.99

KNIGHTS OF THE OLD REPUBLIC
Volume One: Commencement
ISBN 978-1-59307-640-5 | $18.99

Volume Two: Flashpoint
ISBN 978-1-59307-761-7 | $18.99

Volume Three: Days of Fear, Nights of Anger
ISBN 978-1-59307-867-6 | $18.99

Volume Four: Daze of Hate, Knights of Suffering
ISBN 978-1-59582-208-6 | $18.99

Volume Six: Vindication
ISBN 978-1-59582-274-1 | $19.99

Volume Seven: Dueling Ambitions
ISBN 978-1-59582-348-9 | $18.99

Volume Eight: Destroyer
ISBN 978-1-59582-419-6 | $17.99

REBELLION
Volume One: My Brother, My Enemy
ISBN 978-1-59307-711-2 | $14.99

Volume Two: The Ahakista Gambit
ISBN 978-1-59307-890-4 | $17.99

Volume Three: Small Victories
ISBN 978-1-59582-166-9 | $12.99

LEGACY
Volume One: Broken
ISBN 978-1-59307-716-7 | $17.99

Volume Two: Shards
ISBN 978-1-59307-879-9 | $19.99

Volume Three: Claws of the Dragon
ISBN 978-1-59307-946-8 | $17.99

Volume Four: Alliance
ISBN 978-1-59582-223-9 | $15.99

Volume Five: The Hidden Temple
ISBN 978-1-59582-224-6 | $15.99

Volume Seven: Storms
ISBN 978-1-59582-350-2 | $17.99

Volume Eight: Tatooine
ISBN 978-1-59582-414-1 | $17.99

DARK TIMES
Volume One: The Path to Nowhere
ISBN 978-1-59307-792-1 | $17.99

Volume Two: Parallels
ISBN 978-1-59307-945-1 | $17.99

Volume Four: Blue Harvest
ISBN 978-1-59582-264-2 | $17.99

darkhorse.com
AVAILABLE AT YOUR LOCAL COMICS SHOP OR BOOKSTORE.
TO FIND A COMICS SHOP IN YOUR AREA, CALL 1-888-266-4226
For more information or to order direct: On the web: darkhorse.com
E-mail: mailorder@darkhorse.com • Phone: 1-800-862-0052 Mon.–Fri.
9 AM to 5 PM Pacific Time. STAR WARS © 2004–2010 Lucasfilm Ltd. & ™ (BL8005)